Raphael
    Richard Wagner

TWAYNE'S WORLD AUTHORS SERIES

A Survey of the World's Literature

Sylvia E. Bowman, Indiana University

GENERAL EDITOR

GERMANY

Ulrich Weisstein, Indiana University

EDITOR

Richard Wagner

(TWAS 77)

TWAYNE'S WORLD AUTHORS SERIES (TWAS)

*The purpose of TWAS is to survey the major writers
—novelists, dramatists, historians, poets, philosophers,
and critics—of the nations of the world. Among the
national literatures covered are those of Australia,
Canada, China, Eastern Europe, France, Germany,
Greece, India, Italy, Japan, Latin America, New Zea-
land, Poland, Russia, Scandinavia, Spain, and the
African nations, as well as Hebrew, Yiddish, and
Latin Classical literatures. This survey is comple-
mented by Twayne's United States Authors Series
and English Authors Series.*

*The intent of each volume in these series is to present
a critical-analytical study of the works of the writer;
to include biographical and historical material that
may be necessary for understanding, appreciation,
and critical appraisal of the writer; and to present all
material in clear, concise English—but not to vitiate
the scholarly content of the work by doing so.*

Richard Wagner

By ROBERT RAPHAEL

Queens College

Twayne Publishers, Inc. :: New York

In Memory of Wieland Wagner

Preface

AMONG professional students of literature, Richard Wagner's status continues to be problematical not only because of the composite nature of his art, but also due to the fact that he conceived of himself and wrote as an esthetician as well as social and political philosopher. As a consequence, the prevailing attitude toward the literary Wagner has remained confused, if not contentious or even disdainful, the result being that Wagner, the dramatist of ideas, has been either ignored or misunderstood. The present work seeks to cast this aspect of Wagner into large relief.

Even if the poetic style of his music dramas is open to criticism, Wagner's dramatic thinking is not. Yet he remains considerably neglected, and often thoroughly misconstrued, as an artist who disclosed some highly pertinent and disturbing notions about the human situation, and whose works have vividly contributed to the stream of Western culture.

Despite the fact that Wagner's significance and popularity rest almost entirely on the musical aspect of his creations, the study at hand hopes to call attention to his enormous creativity from another angle, that of Richard Wagner as an intellectual and perceptive cultural analyst who innovated bracing myths that can be seen to function as total metaphors for our mortal condition. These myths do, in fact, reveal the predicament of Romantic European civilization in all its major phases, at least as Wagner glimpsed it with his profound, unblinking gaze.

Accordingly, this study endeavors to divulge the very organic continuity of ideas throughout Wagner's work, as they can be seen to evolve from drama to drama in strict chronological order of genesis. Musical aspects are brought to light only whenever they shed additional light on the evolution of the man or the dramatist in connection with his ideas in their entirety.

All translations from the German are by the author.

ROBERT RAPHAEL

New York City

Contents

Contents

Chronology

1813 Richard Wagner is born at Leipzig, May 22. His father dies in November.

1814 Wagner's mother weds the actor and poet Ludwig Geyer, who dies in 1821. The family moves to Dresden.

1827 Return to Leipzig. Start of serious musical studies. First amateur works.

1832 Concludes six months of advanced musical training at Leipzig University. First serious compositions published and performed. *Die Hochzeit* written.

1833 Stage experience at Würzburg. Writes *Die Feen.*

1834 Director of theater in Magdeburg, where he remains until 1836.

1836 *Das Liebesverbot* receives one performance at Magdeburg. Marries Minna Planer.

1837 Director of theater in Riga, Latvia (then as now part of Russia). First two acts of *Rienzi.*

1839 Flees to Paris via London (in July) because of debts.

1840 Financial distress and artistic disappointment in Paris. *Rienzi* completed.

1841 Composes *The Flying Dutchman* in seven weeks. Hears music of Berlioz. Meets Heine, Liszt, and Meyerbeer.

1842 *Rienzi* commissioned at Dresden and performed on October 20. *The Flying Dutchman* produced on January 2, 1843. Becomes Court Conductor at Dresden.

1845 *Tannhäuser* performed. First sketch for *Die Meistersinger.*

1848 *Lohengrin* completed. Sketch for a Nibelung myth.

1849 Participates in Dresden revolt, narrowly avoiding arrest. Flees to Switzerland.

1850 *Lohengrin* performed under Franz Liszt at Weimar.

1852 *Der Ring des Nibelungen* completed as a drama.

1853 Composition of *Das Rheingold.*

1856   *Die Walküre* finished. *Siegfried* begun.

1857   *Siegfried* laid aside at end of Act Two. *Tristan und Isolde* begun.

1858   Act Two *of Tristan* written in Venice; the entire work completed in 1859.

1861   Paris version of *Tannhäuser.* Hears *Lohengrin* for the first time in Vienna.

1864   Invited by King Ludwig II of Bavaria. Moves to Munich in May.

1865   Production of *Tristan* in Munich under Hans von Bülow, June 10.

1866   Moves to new home, "Triebschen," in Lucerne, Switzerland. Lives with Cosima von Bülow, Liszt's daughter. Minna dies in Dresden.

1868   *Die Meistersinger* first produced in Munich. Meets the young Nietzsche at Leipzig.

1869   First performance of *Rheingold* in Munich. Siegfried born to Cosima. Composition of *Siegfried,* Act Three. *Götterdämmerung* begun.

1870   First *Walküre* in Munich. Marries Cosima on the King's birthday.

1872   Moves to Bayreuth. Construction of Festspielhaus begun.

1874   Moves to Bayreuth home, "Wahnfried." *Götterdämmerung* finished.

1876   Initial performance of complete *Ring,* August 13–17.

1877   *Parsifal* started. Conducts in London and is received by Queen Victoria. His health begins to fail.

1882   *Parsifal* completed in Sicily, performed at Bayreuth in July.

1883   Death in Venice on February 13.

CHAPTER 1

Decisive Beginnings

IN all of cultural history, the peculiarly Wagnerian combination of poet-dramatist and composer is virtually without a parallel. Within a span of forty years, throughout the middle decades of the nineteenth century, Richard Wagner fused dramatic conceptions of staggering breadth and depth with music of such astounding novelty and ingeniousness that much of the very shape and sinew of musical tradition were altered and have never again been the same; nor has the lyric stage.

Wagner's beginnings were modest. No one observing his talent up to nearly his thirtieth year could have surmised—at least on the merit of the works performed—what he was to become. He started as a dilettante in those very arts that were to shape the entire course of his career: literature and music; or, more precisely, Shakespeare and Beethoven. It was on the pattern of these two geniuses that Wagner very early aspired to fashion himself. Far different, however, from men of precocious talent, such as Mozart and Schubert, Shelley and Keats, the teen-ager Wagner merely fumbled along yet scarcely groped his way. He completed whatever he set himself to do, and, unlike a number of Romantic artists, left hardly any fragments behind.

At thirteen already he worked out a tragedy on the scale of Shakespeare and the early Goethe. This drama, *Leubald*—with over twenty dramatis personae—saw so many of its characters murdered in the course of a family vendetta that some of them, near the end, had to be revived as ghosts. Two years later, the young man determined to have music for his play, in the manner of Beethoven's for Goethe's historical drama *Egmont*. At this point, then, occurred the unnoticed birth of the artist of whom the world was soon to learn and whom it was never to forget.

Beethoven, Shakespeare, and Goethe: they form a mighty fuse that ignited the young man's determination to make himself

into a dramatic composer. He visualized Beethoven as an ele-
vated, supernatural being who merged inevitably with his vision
of the divine Shakespeare.[1]

With ambitions leaping ahead of his capabilities—but not far—
Wagner, by 1829, was composing one piece of music after the
other. A particular selection was transcribed quite fantastically in
blue, red, and black ink, each color imbued with a visionary and
mystic significance of its own, and each one meant for a different
section of the orchestra. The piece, an overture in B flat major,
actually received a performance—Wagner's very first—at a Leipzig concert on Christmas Day, 1830. In the same year, Wagner
did something nobody had thought of doing before—a truly virtuoso feat—namely, copying out the full score of Beethoven's
Ninth Symphony (in those days very scantily known) and ar-
ranging that huge work for piano solo. He sent the product off to
a publisher, and was paid with the score of the composer's *Missa
Solemnis*. Even now he was becoming what many a Romantic
artist of that epoch was only dreaming about: the unique visionary artist and virtuoso in one. Somehow, in the womb of his imagination, the whole Wagner had already come into being. He was
seventeen.

During the summer of 1832, Wagner wrote his first text intended entirely for music. Inspired by the work of E. T. A. Hoffmann, Germany's popular and influential author of macabre and
high-strung Gothic tales, *Die Hochzeit* (The Wedding) was to remain the only fragment of its kind, with but a chorus and a short
recitative completed in a rather Beethovenesque manner.[2]

In January, 1833, hoping to escape military service in Saxony
and eager to join his brother Albert, Wagner left Leipzig and
moved to Würzburg in Bavaria. Here the young man at a minimal
salary was initiated into the everyday practicalities of stage business by serving throughout that year as chorus director at the
small municipal theater, where his brother was engaged as leading tenor. At the end of that year, Wagner had finished the text
and music of his first complete work for the stage, *Die Feen* (The
Fairies), the fantastic realm of the story being the kind that Hoffmann had recommended for true Romantic opera.[3] Before the
year was out, Wagner had the satisfaction of having excerpts from
it performed at Würzburg with his brother singing a part. Nonetheless, the work as a whole was to remain unproduced in his

lifetime.[4] As he turned twenty-one, Wagner still had no prospects of a career. Indeed, what professional life he enjoyed during the eight years that followed was destined to be sporadic, underpaid, and often humiliating.

For the season of 1834–35, Wagner took on the post of director at the Magdeburg theater. There he remained until 1836, a period which brought two important events: his eventual marriage with the actress Minna Planer, who was more than three years his senior and proved to be a devoted but pedestrian spouse; and the completion of his second stage work, *Das Liebesverbot* (The Ban on Love). With a text culled from Shakespeare's comedy *Measure for Measure*, this opera, despite its youthful exuberance and charm, received only a single, poorly attended performance on March 29, 1836. The work exhibits notions then current and popular among numerous youthful Germans, many of whom considered themselves part of a movement known as "Young Germany." This group disdained the past with its puritanical mores and extolled freedom from convention, as well as the virtues of sensuality. It was the latter which Wagner, in his second opera, emphasized to a degree that caused some contemporaries to view it as licentious, and the Magdeburg police to look at it askance. Accordingly, a new title, "The Novice of Palermo," supplanted the old one given to this "Grand Comic Opera in Two Acts." It is far more grand than comic, however, in the way in which Wagner unmasks the lust and hypocrisy of Friedrich, the ruler who bans lovemaking but has intentions toward the innocent Isabella who, in a rather saintly fashion, renounces the world at the end. Here we have intimations of the lofty Elisabeth in *Tannhäuser*. Not surprisingly, the theme that is casually associated with Isabella's first entrance is taken up once more in *Tannhäuser*, with changed instrumentation, to characterize Elisabeth's holiness.

Wagner's obvious interest in *Das Liebesverbot* lies not in the comedy, which is rather too heavy-handed to seem convincing, but in the serious scenes revolving about Isabella and her implicitly tragic situation. When such moments come, quite predictably, the very best that is in the young Wagner comes to the fore. As Isabella confronts Friedrich and finds her own and her brother's future in jeopardy, we note the Wagnerian stance: the orchestra surges with the ardent theme heard in the overture, while the voices merely *accompany* it in earnest recitative. Each time, in fact, as the drama accumulates serious emotional tension, the orchestra takes control and resolves it. The prospect of a sea of sound hidden beneath a universal stage is no longer embryonic.

After his engagement in Magdeburg had ended, in the spring of 1836, Wagner conducted for a short while in Königsberg, Prussia, before taking on the musical directorship of the theater in Riga. As the overseer of musical life in this Russian provincial town, he scarcely made himself popular. He was starting to move completely away from the notion of the lyric stage as a place of mere entertainment. His growing idealism soon made him unloved by the artists in his charge, as well as by his peers. He harassed the company with endless rehearsals that lasted for hours at a stretch, and insisted on artistic perfection and a dedication that was simply not to be had at that place and time. The large ambitions at work in him gave rise, in turn, to a work of large scope that—four years later—was to constitute the basis of his rise to fame. The first two acts of the five-act setting of Bulwer-Lytton's contemporary English novel *Rienzi* (1835) were finished while Wagner was still in Riga. His perennial financial troubles, however, soon took a fateful hand in the matter, for his debts became so large that he was forced to escape, if for no other reason than to insure his personal safety.[5]

In the year 1839 escape from Russia was apparently no easier than it is today. The details of how, under the real threat of being shot at any moment, Wagner and Minna, together with their very large dog, made their way across the Russian frontier into Prussia, how the fugitives were smuggled aboard the small sailing ship *Thetis* bound for London, and how they almost were shattered by one violent storm after the other, constitute one of the most colorful episodes in a life that was filled with excitement.[6]

The terrifying voyage took well over three weeks. The trio landed at London on August 12, after a trip which, in normal summer weather, should have lasted about ten days. The feeling of the ship's crew of seven, growing stronger with every tempest, was that the shady personality smuggled on board had, indeed, brought upon them all of the extraordinarily evil weather, and that somehow the fugitive was accursed.

This *was* actually the truth, even though it was truth of a kind not one of them could have guessed. The stormy and troubled voyage on the *Thetis* has often been accepted—uncritically but appropriately enough—as having provided Wagner with his first inspiration for the tempestuous and doomed atmosphere of *The Flying Dutchman*. In actual fact, Wagner had already made himself thoroughly familiar with Heine's version of the legend while yet in Riga; and more than likely he had already been dwelling on its scenic possibilities. Possibly, the sheer violence of storm and sea merely became a dramatic focus for all the visions and energies that had been welling up inside him ever since his becoming aware of a new and uncompromising kind of art. *He* was the flying Dutchman, wandering, homeless, and accursed. The harrowing outward event only fed and magnified the high blaze in his inward eye, which now saw the artist's inescapable otherness, his sundering and alienation from society. What Richard Wagner was feeling just at that point in his career was no different from what many other artists were feeling, or had felt, in the Romantic Age. It was the experience of a world without value and meaning, and the urgent need to discover some ground for value, some kind of meaningful relationship that could bridge the gulf between the subjective and the objective world.[7]

Nevertheless, to Wagner at his time of flight, Paris—and with it the dream of a production of *Rienzi* that might give him professional roots and a stable life—appeared for the moment as a golden land. It turned out to be less than that. What began for him as he came to Paris were, in fact, the two-and-a-half most wretched years of his nearly seventy spent on earth. This agonizing period, in what was then the hub of musical civilization, was characterized by illusions ripped to tatters, by his seldom having enough to eat, and by his temporarily ending up in a debtor's prison in late October, 1840.

But the Parisian experiences were hardly all on the debit side. Despite every kind of hardship, Wagner never lost a shred of that incredible self-confidence, regarding his own artistic importance and his own creative powers, that more than once was to help him surmount later trials. Far from giving in to his misery, he completed, by the fall of 1840, not only the last three acts of *Rienzi*, but in addition, during the summer of 1841, he composed the music to his drama *The Dutchman* in a matter of seven weeks.

Finally, Paris proved to be the site of his initial self-awareness as a distinctively German artist who had novel and significant things to say.

CHAPTER 2

Dead End and New Beginning

WITH the acceptance of *Rienzi*, in June 1841, by the Dresden Court Theater rescue came at last and led to the young composer being transported back to the soil where he belonged. The composer arrived in Dresden in the following year, and on the night of October 20, the Richard Wagner of history stepped into view. His "Grand Tragic Opera in Five Acts, after Bulwer's Novel," was an incredible success, quite undimmed by its temporal extension. It was to be the public's first taste of Wagnerian lengths.

The course of the drama was in tune with the "progressive" political and social mood of that day. It was naturally attuned to Wagner's thoughts along those lines, which were anti-clerical, anti-aristocratic, and pro-middle-class. The liberal Cola Rienzi, incensed by his innocent daughter's seduction by an aristocrat and by the evil tyranny of the nobles, drives them out of Rome, with the populace behind him. The medieval Church, however, through excommunication and a pact with the Emperor, finally brings about the hero's downfall.

Despite all its dramatic surge and tragic glamor, *Rienzi* is musical theater with a superficial sheen. Lavishly set, stunningly heroic, with music often stirring and bright, the work is brilliant *grand* opera in every bar. The way for it had been already well prepared by Meyerbeer and Spontini, the "big" opera composers of the time. Yet, *Rienzi* was opera to a Wagnerian tune, and Wagner spun it out to an absolute finish. For him, as for anyone else who listens to it with critical attention, it is obvious that *Rienzi* meant a dead end.

In all likelihood, he had outgrown *Rienzi*'s furthest esthetic limits even as he put the final touches to it while still in Paris. He displays an exuberant mastery of all technical means; there is a thorough professionalism about the score that attests to this. From sheer virtuosity and talent, the twenty-seven-year-old hollows out the entire stance and style of the genre he works in. The step that follows *Rienzi*, therefore, is taken not by default, but solely out of necessity.

I *The Nature of Romanticism*

The initial performance of *The Flying Dutchman* (*Der fliegende Holländer*) on January 2, 1843, turned out, not surprisingly, to be less than a moderate success. The rather inadequate performance is not, in itself, sufficient to explain the reason.[1] In point of fact, the Dresden audience was confronting the real Wagner for the first time. Expecting another feat like *Rienzi*, many Dresdeners were bewildered and disappointed.

Actually, it was not the music that obstructed the ready reception of the work. In spite of somber passages with no discernible melody (one hears complaints about that even now), the music still moves very much along patterns long laid out and familiar. It was rather the peculiar story, with all its gloom and its psychological fissures, that set a chill and made the going rough. The fact of the matter was that Wagner had turned into a genuine Romantic and, like most Romantics on advanced cultural levels, had started to twist himself inside out, and occasionally even upside down. First of all—and this point was crucial—he found himself no longer able merely to "set" his music to ready-made plays or novels, as nearly all opera composers do, and have always done.[2] Instead, Wagner now began to write his own dramas—really dramatic myths—and to compose music for them, as it were, from the inside. Music and drama now form an indivisible unit, and thus arose the inimitable Wagnerian working method: the full text of the drama is written down to *music that is already there*.

In actuality, Wagnerian verse, when it is good, can stand on its own intrinsic literary merits; at its worst, it still remains fully adequate to Wagner's *musical* purposes which, as a rule, he already had in mind while setting down his words. The overriding musical design did, in fact, dictate the general textual forms in which the dramas were ultimately conceived. This fact accounts, in part, for the striking diversity of versification forms throughout his ten major works. It helps explain why no one of them is really like the other; why, for example, *Tristan's* pre-Expressionistic telegrammatic style is so markedly different from that of the *Ring* with its conspicuously, and sometimes clumsily, alliterative verse, and why the versification of *Die Meistersinger* differs from all the others in its sixteenth-century *Knittelvers,* which closely models the verse forms of the historical Hans Sachs. On the other hand, Wagner's final work, *Parsifal,* like the three major dramas before the *Ring,* is carefully wrought in varied rhyme schemes.

It might be an interesting experiment to see some of Wagner's works, especially the *Ring,* performed solely as dramas without the music. Morse Peckham has suggested that this might indeed be successfully done. In this author's opinion, however, the lasting success of such an experiment, as valid and as interesting as it may appear, would be open to serious question.

With his accustomed eloquence where Wagner was concerned, Thomas Mann described the process, and the result, succinctly when he wrote that "the texts about which the music entwines, thus filling them with dramatic blood, are not literature, but the music *is.*" [3] Wagner is, in Mann's words, "the savior of the opera through the myth." [4] Beginning with *The Flying Dutchman,* he becomes a mythologist in order to deal with cultural problems in terms of a metaphorical treatment of legend or history. This is also a Romantic solution, for the Romantic artist feels impelled to exploit any myth, any tradition, or history itself, as supreme fiction. But what is a Romantic? Specifically, what was the Romantic cultural situation in which the problem of the Dutchman had to be resolved? For it is always this situation which inevitably shapes the work-to-be.

The wrong, old-fashioned way of discussing Romanticism in *The Flying Dutchman* is to begin by listing its "Romantic" attributes, such as the ship with black masts and blood-red sails, its ghostly crew, the clairvoyant dreams, the hysterical and trance-like Senta, or the eerie figure of the Dutchman himself. Once these things are named, we learn something about qualities labeled Gothic but next to nothing about the ways in which Wagner's drama is Romantic. We can never say what Romanticism is, because it *is* not anything; we can only talk about how Romanticism *works.* From that point, we might say that *The Flying Dutchman* is indeed Romantic, since, within it, Wagner's ideas and symbols *function* deliberately in a fashion characteristic of the way in which other symbols function in other Romantic works which attempt to solve the same general problem and face the same dilemma that confounds Wagner. The dilemma was this: how can one negate the value and meaningfulness of society, and yet manage to enter it and survive in it? This profound sense of life without meaning, of a world void of all value, of identity lost and wretched, marks clearly the death of Enlightenment views, which held that men could adapt to a divine universe radiant with order and value; it also signals the birth of the nineteenth-century orientation. The novel distinction in the minds of the few culturally advanced individuals, the true Romantics, betokened a shift of view and purpose that was to prove as vast and seminal for culture as the invention of the wheel. The explosion of the Enlightenment and pre-Enlightenment world first occurred in Goethe's novel *Werther* (1774), but its rumblings are heard much later, and perhaps more typically, in such things as Byron's *Cain* and *Manfred,* as well as in the various forms of the story of the Flying Dutchman.

The first cultural changes that mark the primary stages of what we call Romanticism are described by Morse Peckham:

Rebirth, restoration, rediscovery of value for these men came from within, came from, they felt, the ultimate depths of the mind itself, from its very nature and structure. At a stroke mind was sundered from nature, Subject from Object, the Self from the role, which was seen at best as the means of realizing the Self, and at worst, as the instrument whereby nature violated the Self. The Romantic experienced a sense of profound isolation within the world and an equally terrifying alienation from society. These two experiences, metaphysical isolation and social alienation—they are of course two different modes of the same perception—were the distinguishing signs of the Romantic, and they are to this day. To symbolize that isolation and alienation and simultaneously to assert the Self as the source of order, meaning, value, and identity, became one task of the Romantic personality. To find a ground for value, identity, meaning, order, became the other task.[5]

The development of the anti-role, therefore, became the one most essential and seminal innovation of the Romantic, the very precondition for a new search for value. The creation of anti-roles symbolizes how the Self alone becomes the source of value, and how this sense of identity, at the same time, is unshackled from all previous traditional and prescribed roles, whether from nature, God, or society.

The earliest kind of anti-role—the basic type from which all others emerge—is that of the wandering outcast, the mysterious criminal whose crimes may be unmentioned or unmentionable. His role refuses to be integrated into anything, including the social structure. The classic type is the Byronic Hero, or the Flying Dutchman. In the Wagnerian version, as in others preceding it, the Dutchman is condemned to sail the seven seas for eternity as a punishment for his blasphemy.[6] But in Wagner's treatment a salient point, which differs from earlier versions, except Heine's (from which it was derived), is the period of grace allowed to the Dutchman every seven years. During these rare intervals he is permitted to go ashore, so that he might find a woman who will bring him final salvation by being *dedicated* to him even unto death. "Faithful" or "true unto death" are hardly good renditions of Wagner's *Treue*. Utter dedication through empathy comes perhaps closest to an adequate translation of the word. In the Romantic hue of things, pervasive empathy can be seen as the basis for all morality, and as the cohesive element throughout the social structure. In Richard Wagner, at this stage and for the rest of his life, it is the vital touchstone for human relationships, the premise of salvation.

II The Flying Dutchman: *The Outcast and Society, Part I*

In contradistinction to the works to come, *The Flying Dutchman* has obvious correspondences in Wagner's life. Between 1839 and 1842, Wagner felt indeed cast out and isolated from society, and during those Riga and Paris years he literally tried to re-enter it. In addition, it is not by chance that in the first draft of the opera the heroine's name was Minna. And yet the very personal foundation of the work leads to no personal resolution, to no actual confrontation with society. The solution remains, in fact, so open-ended that it can be regarded as no solution whatever to the ultimate Romantic dilemma of re-entry. At the last, *The Flying Dutchman* turns out to be not at all concerned with re-entry; it is concerned with empathy, expressed by the words *Treue* and *Mitleid*, and how empathy is incarnated to a degree that it may function as an anti-role, quite apart from the need to re-enter and adapt to a deceptive world that violates its members even while absorbing them into a system of roles.

With another seven-year term of ocean-wandering completed, the Dutchman once more makes port in search of salvation. In a Norwegian village he meets the seafarer Daland, who has a daughter for sale, especially after he discovers that the Dutchman's ship is richly laden with treasure. "She shall be your wife if she pleases you," Daland tells the hopeful outcast. The Dutchman regards Daland's offer as at least one more chance of finding his "angel of salvation" and ending his eternal woe.

Before the Dutchman's arrival, Daland's daughter sits entranced, as often in the past, before a portrait of the accursed man. To her circle of female friends Senta tells her hopes of bringing the Dutchman redemption by showing him fidelity even to death. It is the ballad of the Flying Dutchman which she sings, and has sung before to the horror of her friends—but particularly of Erik, who hopes that Senta will intercede with her father so that they might marry. Soon Erik reminds Senta of this fact and of his revulsion toward what seems to be her childish infatuation with a mere picture and a legend. Senta insists, however, that her empathy (*Teilnahme*) for the unhappy man has guided all her feelings and thoughts. When Erik asks whether the suffering she has caused *him* should not move her more, Senta demands to know what compared to that of the doomed man his torment can be.

Erik thereupon relates a clairvoyant dream, in which he saw Senta rush into the Dutchman's arms and kiss him eagerly before they sailed off forever. It is a dream into which Senta herself interpolates details; for she, too, has dreamt it.

Senta has rejected Erik's *Treue* decisively, since it is based on the fidelity of conventional matrimony and on the erotic feelings inherent in a social role. The kind of *Treue* which motivates Senta lies on an utterly different plane. It springs from what the German philosopher Schopenhauer has called "die Erkenntnis des fremden Leidens," *the perception of another's suffering* that moves one to genuine deeds of love. "Genuine love," Schopenhauer insists, "by its very nature is compassion (*Mitleid*), and every sort of love which does not stem from compassion is egocentric." [7] Senta's rejection of Erik can be viewed, therefore, not only as the rejection of a social mask, but also as a discarding of egocentricity.

In the end, Senta refuses to play any role expected of her by her father, by friends, or by Erik. Instead, she remains in the trance of a saint, absorbed, as with an obsession, in the contemplation of value and its single mission, and with the saint's disregard of society and worldly things. She is, however, a Romantic saint. By entering the same spiritual wasteland as the Dutchman, she accepts alienation. She even seeks it, for in this way she learns to derive value from the Self alone. Thus, being steeped in the Dutchman's portrait and the legend of his doomed alienation is tantamount to her own situation and symbolizes her own attitude toward the Self. It may be seen that, at this stage of Wagnerian Romanticism, the Subject shuns the Object (the world) altogether; instead, it turns in upon itself in order to feed on itself in an orgy of consummation, simply because it has no choice. Dreams, trances, and clairvoyance are true Romantic symbolizations of the notion that all value and all meaningful reality can come solely from the most profound levels of the personality and must originate wholly within the deep resources of the mind.

It is natural for Senta to be in a profound trance when she actually confronts the seaman. She hears him relate that it is not "love" which drives him forth in an endless search; it is rather "the yearning for salvation." In return, Senta tells him how her life has become "a wondrous dreaming," and how the reality she has endured seems like "a world of deception." She then asks whether the voice of compassion *can* deceive her, adding that through her the Dutchman will at last find redemption.

This scene, the solid core of the drama, provides a lucid Wagnerian example of what Peckham considers to be the primary stage of the Romantics, in which rebirth, salvation, and the discovery of value emerge from within, from "the ultimate depths of the mind itself, from its very nature and structure." Senta's striking perception of value arising exclusively from the Self in jarring contrast to the void of the world, and her discovery that this vision is confirmed by the Dutchman's very existence and his whole fate, betoken a novel and exciting mode of experience that she can indeed compare to a wonderful dream.

But the Dutchman has further revelations in store. Near the conclusion of the drama, as he is about to set forth on yet another seven-year voyage, once more in despair of finding genuine empathy that will set him free, he reveals his identity to the villagers as well as to Senta. He tells them that he is the condemned Flying Dutchman and emphasizes the transcendental conditions and terms of his fate and his salvation: only a woman true to death can redeem him. Senta has actually done so, he asserts, yet not before God Eternal; and *this* will save *her*. Not fulfilling this ultimate condition, he adds, has hitherto caused many a woman to fall victim to his curse.

So goes the myth which Wagner uses, but which he exploits with a characteristic twist. The seaman announces that Senta, in spite of all the terms set by God and the devil in the past, will now *be saved anyway*, because she has empathy. With that the Dutchman suddenly departs, precisely as he had arrived (just as Lohengrin was later to do), in his spectral ship with its eerie crew.

What this really means, and what proves Wagner to be employing the cultural symbolism of the Romantics, is that his solution lies completely outside the traditional myth. At the end, Wagner simply discards important aspects of the myth so that he may serve his own mythology all the better. In his version of the myth, empathy surmounts not merely the deceptive world of masks and roles; it transfigures alienation also by surpassing the very myth in which the dramatist operates. This occurs as soon as the Dutchman learns to show the same amount of empathy toward his potential victim as he demands from her, and which she has in fact shown. In the end, he has released her from doom without—and here lies the rub—expecting anything from her in return.

In a flash of dramatic intensity, Senta replies to the Dutchman's display of genuine empathy by proclaiming that she is in truth his angel of salvation. As the shattered man sails off, she proves this by tossing herself from a cliff into the sea. In this way, she becomes his, and her own, angel of death. That is to say, by fleeing the world and drifting forever in a limbo, two Selves merely cancel each other out, empathy or not. At the last, it is not only the problem of re-entry which remains unsolved; the question also remains whether empathy can be used as an instrument for living in the real world. It was many, many years before Wagner provided an answer.

III   Tannhäuser: *The Outcast and Society, Part Two*

As early as April, 1842, upon his return to Germany, Wagner became engrossed in what was to be the next step beyond the

Dutchman problem. It turned out to be more of a continuation than any real answer to it. Only in the following spring, when his name was beginning to be familiar in Germany, did he set out to create the poem he called *Der Venusberg*, but which soon was to acquire fame as *Tannhäuser*.[8]

One might wonder why did Wagner's key notions on this subject hover doggedly about the mountain of Venus, which, according to popular and Christian tradition, was the ill-reputed abode of the Love Goddess. The Venusberg is an accursed place, since it defies all religious and social authority and negates in every way the whole anti-sexual tradition of the Christian West. Just being there is obviously an unspeakable crime, and functions for Wagner in precisely the same fashion as the Dutchman's blasphemy. Tannhäuser, therefore, begins as the second mysterious criminal whose transgression is difficult to explain and impossible to expiate.

As the action commences, Tannhäuser yearns to flee from Venus and her hothouse of charms. He wishes to plunge back into open nature, see the moon and stars, and listen once more to the song of birds. He entreats the Goddess of Love with his lyre and his song to allow him again to experience the world's natural beauty.

Unlike his stormy and eerie predecessor, Tannhäuser the artist yearns to re-enter society in one piece. He is not longing for salvation through a woman's *Treue*. Instead, the singer starts out by being torn between extremes of sensual intoxication and the remorse brought on by most proper feelings of Christian guilt. His redemption, he tells the irate Venus as he leaves, resides in the Virgin Mary.

In a sunny meadow beneath the Wartburg castle, which represents "decent" society, the vagrant releases his contrition at the foot of a wayside crucifix and tastes the joy with a bitter edge that comes from identifying, after a long interval, with a world familiar and a morality almost forgotten. Temporarily, he ceases to feel his isolation and alienation. Especially so when Wartburg friends, Wolfram von Eschenbach among them, announce that his beloved Elisabeth has shunned their company since his departure. Without him and his song, their world has become meaningless for her.

The mere name of the saintly Elisabeth causes Tannhäuser's

thoughts to glow with the finest memories of his former life at the Wartburg; so much so that he consents to return to the castle, if only to be reunited with Elisabeth. Society, quite obviously, is without value to each in the absence of the other. The "bold singer" is happily rejoined with Elisabeth, but is cryptic about his whereabouts in the intervening years. Elisabeth, in any case, is mature and intuitive enough to suspect the truth. Nonetheless, as Tannhäuser enters the Wartburg song contest he is still the good boy returned home, and his prospects of actual marriage to Elisabeth seem bright. In this contest, the song competition of Minnesingers that was actually held in 1207, Tannhäuser's predicament in society is neatly revealed. Here, too, the Wagnerian myth becomes superimposed on the hoary legend of "der Danhuser," the wayward minstrel of medieval times.

In the presence of Count Hermann and the nobility assembled for the occasion, Wolfram von Eschenbach opens by expounding the courtly view of love as the worship of the "virtue" of the admired lady, hinting at eroticism solely through euphemism and metaphor, if at all. Yet Tannhäuser answers his friend with a verse that divulges the thirst for sensuality as a significant layer of any "true" affection. In the code book of courtly love, however, this is affection of the "false" type: one must "drink at the fountain with his heart," admonishes Walter von der Vogelweide, "*not* with the lips." Tannhäuser will have nothing of Walter's sterile fountain. In joyful instinct and in pleasure alone he recognizes love.

Throughout this scene of contention, a strong conflict has been mounting within Elisabeth who, from the start, understands the meaning of her minstrel's praise of yearning as the true nature of love. She shyly withholds her approval only because of the cold attitude of the others. At this point, Wagner could give no more graphic symbolization of the profound rift separating genuine feeling and empathy from the superficial and repressive society of the Wartburg. The incipient bond between Tannhäuser and Elisabeth is completely out of joint in this false atmosphere. But Tannhäuser, having grown increasingly impatient with the platitudes he has been forced to hear, jumps up in rebellion and bursts out against the chant-like phrases of his colleagues. Quickly and arrogantly he sings forth in praise of Venus and her erotic magic, and challenges "the poor creatures who have never enjoyed real love" to move into the Venusberg. The entire assembly is instantly thrown into such fury that only the physical intercession of Elisabeth is able to prevent Tannhäuser from being run through by the courtiers' weapons. If up to this point the heroine felt merely empathy, she has now a compassionate understanding of the hero that guides her every action. She becomes a wall of empathy separating the anger of Wartburg society from the prostrate and now totally alienated man who violently spurned the Wartburg's most precious illusion. Even if the self-righteous annoyance of the courtiers is scarcely transformed by Elisabeth's supreme example of compassion for the sinner who just dealt her a virtual "death-blow," her insistence that "*they* are not his judges," and that now God speaks through her, pulls their emotions little by little over to Elisabeth's side. "The Savior," she quietly cautions, "suffered once for him too."

Now regarding the heroine as "an angel who descended from the bright heavens to proclaim God's holy counsel," the assembly is willing to forget and forgive. But solely according to the law's stringent letter which demands that sins the like of Tannhäuser's be absolved by the authority of the Church alone, and by the Pope in Rome, precisely as the Landgraf announces. Tannhäuser must now undertake the long journey there in order to obtain forgiveness. As the act closes, Tannhäuser rushes out to join a band of pilgrims who are passing by, bound for Rome.

In the third act, the mendacity of society becomes patent: its sentimental and spurious illusions can be seen to extend all the way from the Wartburg to Rome, and back again. Below the castle, Elisabeth awaits Tannhäuser's arrival, with the other pilgrims, from the Holy City. As they pass by, he is not among them; she fears now that he will never return. Praying to the Virgin in despair, Elisabeth says that "whenever a sinful desire, a worldly yearning took seed in me, I wrestled with a host of torments that I might slay such feelings."

> Wenn je ein sündiges Verlangen,
> ein weltlich Sehnen keimt' in mir,—
> so rang ich unter tausend Schmerzen,
> dass ich es töt' in meinem Herzen.

She hopes, nevertheless, that even though she was not able to amend every fault, the Lord will receive her out of mercy *in spite of this:*

Doch, konnt' ich jeden Fehl nicht büssen,
so nimm dich gnädig meiner an . . .

Apparently, Elisabeth is wrenched by the same proscribed emotions that have brought Tannhäuser to his ruin. Her hope that she be saved anyway, in spite of everything, points to a very revealing connection with Wagner's turn of thought in *The Flying Dutchman*. Recalling that the Dutchman, out of empathy, announced that Senta would be saved despite her not fulfilling the terms set by God, we realize that Elisabeth's aspirations function the same way. If God accepts her in His mercy in spite of her failings, she may save her loved one on earth *now*. Wagner's stage directions underscore that fact: when Elisabeth leaves the scene the indication is that "her path leads toward heaven where she has a high office to perform."

For both Elisabeth and her doomed sinner salvation would seem to come in the same way as it did for Senta and the Dutchman. Both couples are saved beyond the framework of the legend which, in Tannhäuser's case, is a Christian one. But already at this point Wagner sees all legends and mythologies, whether Christian or not, as being equivalent. Thus, Elisabeth and Tannhäuser are "saved" by default, which is like saying that they are not saved at all. Sharing Tannhäuser's socially unacceptable eroticism, Elisabeth feels that society is not worth the trouble of coming to terms with. Wagner clearly implies that the values which rend the heroine apart are as sick as they are pernicious. This is the major difference between *Tannhäuser* and *The Flying Dutchman*. The earlier work does not examine or condemn society with anything like the scrutiny that prevails here. What salvation does come about, therefore, is one of non-action, and non-being.

When Tannhäuser returns from Rome, the possibilities for his salvation are even more doubtful than Elisabeth's. Wolfram asks the dejected pilgrim to relate his experiences in Rome, adding that he is roused to "a deep compassion" for Tannhäuser. Wagner makes his point here. For the hero reacts with amazement to his friend's concern by exclaiming: "What? Are you not against me?" To which Wolfram gives the revealing reply: "I never was, *so long as I believed you were pious!*" (italics mine). The distance separating Wolfram's notion of empathy from Elisabeth's is greater yet than that between Erik's and Senta's idea of *Treue*.

Tannhäuser's narration completes Wagner's condemnation of the moral authority of the Wartburg, and everything it represents. Filled with piety and genuine self-abasement, Tannhäuser relates how he journeyed to Rome. Along with all the others, he sought *him*, hoping to get his blessing and absolution. But the Pope, learning of his sojourn at the Venusberg, condemns him outright and denies him final absolution with words that proclaim Tannhäuser's excommunication and eternal damnation. At this point, we would be surprised if Wagner were to have it turn out any other way. Tannhäuser's alienation is complete. He sees that it is useless to attempt to enter a society that is hardly worth entering. And he tells Wolfram that the lovely songs announcing grace for all the others only repelled him and blew icy blasts through his heart. In the end, Tannhäuser wants to go back to Venus. The hell of the Venusberg, although tiresome, was at least real and free of falsehood. And in that realm at least he will be welcome. Venus appears in order to greet him and nearly succeeds in bringing him back, until Wolfram mentions the name Elisabeth once more. The Goddess of Love evaporates, and in her place the funeral procession of Elisabeth winds down the hill. Tannhäuser kneels by the coffin, and with the words "Saintly Elisabeth, pray for me!" the minstrel sinks down dead on her bier.

In the end, Tannhäuser is redeemed in spite of himself because, just as Wolfram observes, "your angel prayed for you at God's throne, and is heard." The chorus concluding the work also proclaims salvation by announcing that the pilgrim staff of Tannhäuser, "which had remained barren in the hand of priests," has just sprouted green shoots. It is the miracle worked by Elisabeth's compassion.

Tannhäuser's attempts to re-enter society from a world below are no more successful than were those of the Flying Dutchman. This sinner's redemption, like that of the outcast seaman's, has to be brought about by a woman within society whose empathy, however, reaches beyond Christianity's and society's illusions about love and proper behavior in order to stretch far enough for them both. But this outcome is tantamount to denying any value whatever to the world. It provides no satisfactory solution simply because, as Wagner now came to realize, the problem of re-entry cannot be solved. You cannot enter a society that does not exist. That is to say, one longs to enter society to regain meaning and order; yet if one denies these things to society, there remains no valuable structure to re-enter. Society, as it exists, offers the alienated Romantic hero no opportunity for the recovery of value. All along—ever since the *Rienzi* and Paris years—the certainty of this had begun to seethe in the Wagnerian mind. That is why, with the completion of the *Tannhäuser* score in April, 1845, Wagner suddenly attacked the whole problem of Romantic alienation upside down. He broke off his massive isolation in order to enter society in a new way.

IV The Impossibility of Salvation

If society is not worth entering, then perhaps it can be ennobled, transfigured, and somehow redeemed. This notion undoubtedly occurred to Wagner along with his first conception of *Lohengrin* in 1845. If Tannhäuser could be saved in spite of Christianity, its morality and its institutions, why might not a superior being, on the basis of his own transcendental authority, rescue Christian society? He would enter society again, not from below but from above. In *Lohengrin,* Wagner might just as well have told us that his new hero was not playing The Flying Dutchman or Tannhäuser tonight, but rather a new kind of man, as Lohengrin himself tells Elsa in Act Three: "I come not from night and suffering; I come here from splendor and bliss!"

This time, the hero enters the world in reverse. He descends from Monsalvat, which is a *real* place, a geographical entity, just like the province of Brabant into which he descends. But whereas Brabant is seen as a battleground of Christian and pagan forces, essentially alike in that both seek to control mankind, Monsalvat is a realm of absolute value and purity of action. Its emissary, Lohengrin, who first appears in a swan-driven boat to rescue Elsa from unjust accusations, is as indifferent to the religious needs of Christianity as he is impervious to the attacks of the pagans. He is utterly the artist who lives through Wagner's identification; he is perhaps also the Feuerbachian atheist who pretends to share, and makes use of, the Christian illusions of the "good" Brabantians in order that he might save them.[9]

Indeed, for Wagner all mythologies are equivalent. It is obviously wrong to view *Lohengrin* as a Christian drama, or to consider the hero's mission to be one of defending a young Christian society against the blows of paganism. The drama does work out in favor of the Christians, because this is historically true, and because the pagans clearly espouse reactionary notions. Wagner himself warns us against assuming that his interest in the Lohengrin legend was due to its Christian features or its supernatural implications, when he writes in *A Communication to My Friends:* "The medieval poem brought me the Lohengrin subject in a dusky and mystic form which filled me with mistrust and the kind of antipathy that we feel at the sight of the carved and painted saints along the roads and in the churches of Catholic lands." [10]

Instead, *Lohengrin* presents the myth of Wagner's own essence as a Romantic as well as alienated artist. Thus he descends from the utopia of art, represented by Monsalvat as a legendary world of supreme value, into Christian society, in order to save Elsa, whom he regards as the symbol of the "popular spirit" (*der Geist des Volkes*) and for whom he yearns for "salvation as an artist." [11] Elsa, in other words, is society, and Wagner-Lohengrin is the complete artist who, by his transcendent authority, hopes to redeem it. Lohengrin, in fact, is the total artist Tannhäuser would have become had he been able to introduce the novel and sensual elements of his art into the calcified Wartburg tradition. Tannhäuser may be seen as Wagner in disguise, rebelling against the whole diatonic tradition, and its long list of epigones, with *his* sensuous chromaticism.[12] In *Lohengrin*, with a kind of vengeance, Wagner makes himself omnipotent; but in the end he is forced to observe that re-entry is as impossible as before. In *Lohengrin*, Wagner not only questions the redemptive position of the artist in the world, but also the receptiveness of the social order to art as a transcendent force.

Prior to Lohengrin's arrival in tenth-century Brabant, Ortrud, a reactionary pagan, had gotten rid of Gottfried by witchcraft. Although Gottfried is Elsa's own brother and the heir to the Brabantian throne, Elsa is maliciously accused of the prince's murder by Telramund, who is Ortrud's obedient spouse. Ortrud wants all of Brabant for herself. Elsa, summoned before King Henry to answer the charge, reiterates unswerving faith in the appearance of her savior-knight in bright armor, whom she beheld in a dream and who will rescue her. At last he arrives, to the jubilation of the people and the befuddlement of Telramund and his wife.

Lohengrin descends in a boat pulled by a swan, which is no other than the boy Gottfried, whom Lohengrin has finally rescued from Ortrud by transforming him into such an animal. Yet, by preserving the boy in this disguise is he not acting equivocally? Is he not, in Peckham's words, "exerting arbitrary power? Is he not violating another identity in order to wield social power? And does this not compromise his whole position?" [13]

Lohengrin's rescue of Elsa is by no means unequivocal. She is compelled to prove her absolute faith in her rescuer by never probing into either the source or the nature of his transcendent powers. Elsa must never once question him, Lohengrin gravely cautions, about "where my journey has led from, nor about my name or my identity."

> Nie sollst du mich befragen,
> noch Wissens Sorge tragen,
> woher ich kam der Fahrt,
> noch wie mein Nam' und Art!

Lohengrin's demand for unwavering trust, which may be viewed as a kind of obligatory *Treue*, represents a prohibition which, in fact, leads to coercing Elsa's entire faith as well as her devotion and responsibility toward her intended husband. At the last, however, the golden knight's stricture can be seen as a total violation of Elsa's personality and her volition. Wagner, on the other hand, is trying to say that the transcendent mission of the artist and the workings of his genius are matters that may only be grasped and accepted *on faith*. Obviously, Lohengrin's mission must be finally self-defeating: Faith shall be a matter of personal intuition and empathy, but scarcely one of coercion. The artist clearly cannot redeem society by demanding total recognition and unquestioning faith regarding his significance.

After announcing her unflinching trust in her redeemer and her love for him, Lohengrin expresses his love for Elsa. He then officially proclaims that Elsa is entirely free of any guilt. Lohengrin proves this by winning his trial by combat with Elsa's accuser Telramund. He wins the battle with ease, but graciously spares Telramund's life: the adversary "is to dedicate it to repentance."

Ortrud and her spouse, however, do more than spurn Lohengrin's suggestion. They now deliberately set out to harass Elsa with doubt. Could not, so Ortrud quietly suggests to the girl, her deliverer and prospective mate suddenly leave her by magical

means, just as easily as he once came? The sludge at the bottom of
Ortrud's personality, rooted as it is in relentless paganism and in
her fierce ambition for power, now flows little by little into Elsa.
Soon by perceptible degrees, it throws off the chancy balance of
her *Treue* toward her would-be redeemer, until finally all of her
doubts turn into obsessions. This happens, predictably, when in
Act Three Elsa finds herself at last alone with her "beloved" in the
chamber where their marriage is to consummated. Now, all three
parts of Lohengrin's forbidden question explode from her lips.
This irrevocably compromises Lohengrin's redemptive authority,
as it must. Telramund rushes in to take belated revenge, but he is
slain with a wave of the victor's hand. The knight orders the
corpse borne before the people and the king. He himself will appear there in order publicly to answer Elsa's three queries. Their
happiness (such as it would have been) is dead, Lohengrin laments.

Indeed, Elsa has already glimpsed the fateful swan, her transfigured brother, gliding into Brabant to take away his unearthly
traveller to a transcendental sphere. About his own nature and the
nature of that realm, Lohengrin now has nothing more to conceal.
Before all the people of Brabant, he reveals his source, his nature,
and ultimately his name. He comes from Monsalvat, a realm so
lofty that no mortal eye has perceived it. But the very essence of
that realm's transcendency lies in the holy vessel of the Grail,
chosen servants of which are freed from flaw and evil. The Grail's
immortal glow releases its knights even from the bondage of mor-
tality. Yet once its eternal purpose has been glimpsed—if scarcely
fathomed—by mortals, its blessing must irretrievably vanish in
mortal lives. The vessel's knighthood is also an extension of its
lofty and supreme value, so that once the identity of a Grail servant is grasped, he too must vanish. The golden knight proclaims
that he is such a servant, for he is the son of Parzifal, who wears
the Grail's crown, and his own name is Lohengrin.

Wagner, who subsequently clothes Monsalvat, Parzifal, and the
Grail in wholly different philosophical raiment, shows here how re-
entry—and society's salvation—is never achieved, not because
pure value does not exist and operate, but only because society
remains quite unredeemable, being impervious to supreme values
of any kind. The chasm barring the Romantic artist from the
world yawns deeper than ever before. Lohengrin—and Richard

Wagner—can rely only upon the subliminal alienation of Monsalvat, but in its recesses they may also reflect on the causes that compel them to remain there. It is in such metaphorical recesses that Wagner now begins to conceive the *Ring*.

In actual fact, Wagner has by now solved the difficulty inherent in Lohengrin's re-entry simply by surmounting it; for Lohengrin—far different from either the Dutchman or Tannhäuser—departs from the realm of human society *alive*. If his leavetaking of Elsa can be felt as tragic, it certainly is not fatal. Departing for Monsalvat alive, Lohengrin can still decide what will become of society, but he does in fact guarantee only that its long prevailing but unregenerated patterns shall continue as before. To this end he transforms the swan back into Prince Gottfried and appoints him the future ruler of Brabant. Just before his own disappearance, Lohengrin presents the boy with his horn, sword, and ring—objects that are to loom so importantly throughout the *Ring*. Here, however, they embody the hope merely that Brabant's new and lawful prince will be guided by the values of Lohengrin.

More than this Lohengrin cannot do. This is due to the fact that Lohengrin's transcendental power, which remains the virtual foundation for all his moral authority, became seriously compromised, rather ironically, as soon as he set in movement what he himself refers to as "my good deed." For as part of the assertion of his redemptive power Lohengrin saw fit to violate Gottfried's identity. He did this when he transformed him into a swan. At the end the hero makes clear how Gottfried's resumption of mortal shape had always been contingent upon Elsa's remaining "trustful" for one year. In such fashion, quite obviously, Elsa herself is also violated by being deprived not only of choice but of the exertion of her own moral responsibility as well. Yet if the morality of Monsalvat, with its prohibitions and violations, infringes on Elsa and her brother, Ortrud's lust for power and for the revival of paganism, on the other hand, destroys Elsa's guileless faith just as it shatters her husband's freedom and honor, and finally his life.

By 1848, upon the completion of *Lohengrin*, Wagner ostensibly started to surmise all of the rather drastic consequences of the insights he had already gained. They were insights that probably began to take shape in 1845, propelled by Wagner's mounting disgust with the uncomprehending reactions of both critics and public toward his *Tannhäuser*. Their attitudes in Dresden no doubt helped spark a mood of gloom as well as that profound sense of artistic alienation in which the Lohengrin subject flourished.

The Grail of Monsalvat, and Lohengrin who is the exponent of its supreme source of value, can do nothing, Wagner perceived in 1848, to lighten the heavy shadow of society. At the most it may brighten up its edges, but only for short intervals, if at all. The community remains as unaltered and as unenlightened as before, and Lohengrin must depart because he has no other choice. If there is but a single assurance left, it is that society's rather meaningless continuity will be restored beneath the hopefully wise guardianship of its rightful prince. The community, then, survives, yet it can hardly any longer be seen as adequate.

Actually, Wagner from here on begins to view social man as entirely inadequate, just as previously he began to regard the values of society as thoroughly questionable; despite the prince's restoration, or perhaps because of it. Therefore it is apparent why Wagner, during 1848, started to take a very keen look at the whole structure of social power and its sources. In the huge work he conceived over the next four years, he analyzes the roots and branches of "modern" civilization with such close scrutiny that he ends by confronting—and compels us to confront—practically the entire range of human experience.

CHAPTER 3

The End of the Gods

THE four-and-a-half years that passed between the completion of *Lohengrin* and the final rounding out of the *Ring* poem saw Wagner develop into probably the most perceptive Romanticist working after Schopenhauer and Carlyle and before Strindberg and Nietzsche. Little wonder that *A Sketch for a Nibelung Drama* of 1848 and the drama *Siegfried's Death* written shortly thereafter, seem to have been conceived in a vastly different world from the ultimate rendition, the four-part *Ring of the Nibelung* of 1852.[1] The history of the *Ring* can, in fact, be viewed as the history of the way in which Wagner solved the problem he had seen developing in *Lohengrin,* and in which he actually confronts and works out all the implications of Lohengrin's use of morally equivocal power. By the time he finished it in the fall of 1852, Wagner was able to tell us why society cannot be redeemed by a transcendent morality; or, for that matter, by any morality. He also shows us why it cannot be saved at all.

During the nearly five years it took Wagner to reconceive the world even his own life dramatized the drastic changes within. With his socialist sympathies and his aversion for Saxony's king and its authorities, he participated in the revolt of May, 1849, and was threatened with immediate arrest; he was consequently compelled to flee Dresden with a false passport and to make his way to safety in Switzerland. He was not permitted to reenter Germany until 1860. It is undoubtedly true what he said of himself ten years after the event· "With my poetic conceptions I was constantly so far in advance of my actual experiences that I can consider my moral education almost wholly guided and fixed by these conceptions. The Flying Dutchman, Tannhäuser, Lohengrin, Nibelung, Wotan—were all in my brain before I experienced them."[2] Wagner indicates here that his convictions about the world were always taking shape in the creative recesses of his personality, as symbols, before they became enlarged into the conscious notions about the world that fashioned his own artistic stance toward it. Such inner processes directed him also to ponder lengthily on the relation of art—particularly *his* art—to society. These observations began in the essay *Die Kunst und die Revolution* ("Art and Revolution") in 1849 and continued in *Das Kunstwerk der Zukunft* ("The Art-work of the Future"), *Kunst und Klima* ("Art and Climate"), and *Oper und Drama* ("Opera and Drama") in 1850.

When such "gray clouds of theory" had dissipated, as he later reflected, he felt himself freed to expand the three acts of *Siegfrieds Tod* ("Siegfried's Death") into the four dramas of *Der Ring des Nibelungen*. This task absorbed all his energies during most of 1851 and 1852. Wagner began it by writing *Siegfrieds Tod* backwards; that is, by prefacing it with *Der junge Siegfried* ("The Young Siegfried") and finally with two additional dramas: *Die Walküre* ("The Valkyrie") and *Das Rheingold* ("The Gold of the Rhine"). He then set about rewriting both forward and sideways what was now a tetralogy, expanding and altering especially the latter portions of his immense work. In the long process he also substantially reconceived it. Ultimately, the titles of the last dramas were changed, so that *Der junge Siegfried* became known simply as *Siegfried*, and *Siegfrieds Tod* was transformed into *Die Götterdämmerung*—which, literally translated, means "The Twilight of the Gods" but which in fact should be rendered as "The End of the World."

In order to evaluate Wagner's reordering and profound rethinking of his vast design, it will be important to review his original attitude toward the mythologies he wished to exploit.

The original conception of *Siegfried's Death* was obviously motivated by Wagner's attempt somehow to resolve in an optimistic way the problem faced by Lohengrin. That is to say, Siegfried is seen merely as a mortal instrumentality of the divine Wotan, much in the fashion that Lohengrin was intended to serve the transcendental purposes of Monsalvat. Now it is the transcendent Wotan who causes his young hero to seek a cure for society's ills, before being transported by the Valkyrie Brünnhilde up to him in blissful Walhalla, where henceforth the god will reign unchallenged and everlastingly. Now that Wagner knew why Lohengrin could not remain in Brabant, he thought he had discovered a way that would allow Siegfried and Wotan to survive in an imperishable Walhalla. The solution reflects what might have been the outcome had Lohengrin succeeded with his mission in Brabant. Nonetheless, it poses the same equivocation. Lohengrin's violation of Elsa and her brother is repeated in Wotan's transcendent moral authority, which must exploit its instrument Siegfried in order to insure its own continuity as well as that of social value and order. This does not work, as Wagner soon came to realize. His reaction to the ruling forces of Saxony in 1849 attests to that.

The first evidence of the dramatist's radical shift of view did not, however, come to light until May of 1851, when he made the following significant entry in Act Three of the prose sketch for *The Young Siegfried:* "Wodan and the Wala: end of the gods." A week or so later, he expanded the idea of a "Götterdämmerung" with another entry on the same sheet: "Wodan and the Wala.— Guilt of the gods, and their necessary destruction: Siegfried's mission.—Self-annihilation of the gods." [3] By spring of the following year, Wagner had completed the full prose sketches for *Die Walküre* and *Das Rheingold,* and in a position, at last, to survey his huge plan, he saw a further need of recomposing and adding entire sections, especially in *Siegfried's Death.* Indeed, in order to bring the final two portions of the tetralogy into clear focus with the two dramas that now preceded them he made changes so sweeping that he told Julie Ritter in a letter of February 11, 1853, accompanying his gift of the first privately printed text: "'Siegfried's Death' has turned into something almost wholly new. . . ." [4]

Wagner scarcely exaggerated. The altered and expanded scene with the three Norns, which provides the opening of *Siegfried's Death,* for instance, ran, in its new version, to one-hundred-and-eighty-one lines of text, instead of a mere ninety, almost all of it wholly new material. A totally new foundation for the *Ring* scheme was thus laid down. The fixed point of Wagner's entire concept, the support of the whole mythology of the *Ring,* now lay in this scene of the three Norns at the beginning of the end, not at the actual beginning. In the beginning of *Das Rheingold,* to be sure, the ugly dwarf Alberich commits what has usually been taken for the original crime, from which all further tragedy ensues, when he robs the innocent Rhine maidens of the pure gold at the river bottom. But it is Wotan, Alberich's enemy, who first encroaches on indifferent and meaningless nature, in the belief that he might partially control it and somehow wring from it a kind of permanent value.

As the Norns state in the very beginning, the god Wotan stepped up to the Ash Tree which supports the world, and ripping off one of its branches, he hewed the wood into a spear of earthly power, the *Haft der Welt*. Along the spear the god engraved laws and treaties that were to govern the world. Before being able to do so, Wotan had to drink from a spring at the base of the World Ash, a fountain of wisdom. For the draught the god had to forfeit one of his eyes: He is symbolically half-blind and henceforth, Wagner seems to say, will perceive only one half of the truth. In the course of time—so the Norns continue—the spring from which the god drank sadly gave out, the wound inflicted by Wotan on the Ash Tree caused its leaves to turn sere and fall; and in the fullness of time the mighty tree itself withered and died. This is what the Norns relate at the outset of *Die Götterdämmerung*. Wagner could not be more explicit. Postponing the key to his *Ring* myth until the beginning of the end, Wagner illustrates with a sweeping flashback the very ground of evil, the primeval crime beneath the roots of moral authority in man's Establishment, and the malign cause underlying all of its major social and political acts. By the same stroke he graphically reveals, moreover, the need for its inescapable annihilation, together with that of its chief Wotan who, in the dramatist's phrase, is seen as "the brains of our modern world" (*die Intelligenz der Gegenwart*). For at the last, it is the very wood of the ancient Ash, long lifeless and sere, and now a parable of Nature's violation, that Wotan commands to be hacked down and split into the many logs which are to catch the blaze igniting—with clear poetic justice—his whole world order.[5]

Alberich's later theft of the gold is obviously not the original transgression at all. Ultimately, Alberich's crime can be viewed merely as an extension of Wotan's, whose own initial crime turned into a pervasive force *after* Wagner had drawn up the complete text of *Das Rheingold*. Thus the god's rape of the World Ash, which now becomes the basic immoral act from first to last, may be seen as the first of Wotan's many attempts to assert his control over all of Nature and all of the power inherent in the world. Let us see how this occurs.

Teased into maddening frustration, on account of his ugliness, by the three Rhine maidens, Alberich yearns for the brilliant clump of metal about which they sport, expecially after he learns from them that in possessing it he will achieve power without measure and thereby control the entire world. The attainment of such power, however, they caution him, will be the prize solely of the person who renounces love. In this fashion, Wagner clearly implies what Morse Peckham designates as "the desire for economic power over society [which] takes its origin from the frustration of the human will as it expresses itself in erotic love. Freud himself could say no more on the subject." [6]

But the lovely gold that Alberich rips out of the river bed during the first scene of *Das Rheingold* intrinsically signifies nothing whatever. It is precisely as the river Rhine itself: it is just there. Man, in other words, can never know the world; he may only experience it through desire or frustration, as Alberich does; or else he can seek to control and limit it through imagination and self-governing laws, as Wotan tries to do. Both fail. Power cannot be held morally responsible. In the second scene of *Das Rheingold*, Wotan's attempts to use power responsibly are shown to underline this fact.

I *The Horror of Power*

In the presence of his wife Fricka, beneath the newly-built Walhalla, Wotan proclaims that the mighty fortress will become an impregnable foundation for his eternal power. Along with power shall come masculine honor and everlasting fame. Yet Fricka points out that this is a deception. Her husband would be better guided, she says, by "love and woman's worth," the eternally feminine. On Fricka's lips we recognize the familiar Wagnerian formula for the cohesion of the social bond: empathy is the most valuable aspect of all human emotion and endeavor. It is the most profound level of non-erotic love.

The first explicit indictment of Wotan comes with the entrance of Fasolt and Fafner, the giants with whom the god has contracted to build Walhalla. For their hard toil Wotan has promised them Freia, the goddess of beauty and youth, although never seriously intending to give her to them. When the giants hear that Freia is not for sale, they rightly accuse Wotan of breach of contract. Fasolt points out that Wotan's limited power, along with his treaties and laws, is evidently paradoxical; for self-limiting power is a basic contradiction in terms. Wotan soon finds that he must have *all* the power in his hands, or none.

To begin with, Fasolt reminds him, Wotan's power derives solely from the treaties and laws engraved on the spear; they alone make him what he thinks he is. Through these laws, in fact, Wotan originally forced the giants to accept *his* kind of peace. Before that they were free men. Under the present conditions, Fasolt continues, he curses all of Wotan's wisdom and yearns to escape from his brand of "peace" if such be the way the god honors contracts. A stupid giant, he ironically adds, is forced to say these facts to Wotan. This searing revelation is, as we shall see, only the first challenge to Wotan's very position.

Now the brother giants threaten to rob Freia from the gods unless Wotan pays them. But the thunder-god Donner, enraged at the notion of lovely Freia as a hostage, menaces the pair with his weighty hammer. Here Wotan's self-imposed limitations are exposed. He intervenes between Donner and the giants, exclaiming that nothing shall be done through force. His spear protects order and law, and all acts must be legal. Wotan's insistence on strict legality at this point—and from now on—turns out to be vacuous. In actual fact, Wotan quickly discovers the full paradox of his power. At this point he recalls that Loge, the god of fire, whom he has also tamed through the laws engraved on the spear, can come to his aid with cunning and deceit. Wotan, in other words, finds himself so obscured in the shambles of his own trickery that only Loge's clever advice can save him.

From the crafty fire-god Wotan hears the first news of Alberich's theft of the Rhine gold. Loge also informs him how the wretch renounced human love in order to amass untold-of riches and, with time, to win the whole world for himself. This he will do, Loge warns, through the all-powerful ring now being fashioned by him from the stolen gold. "I *must* have the ring!" Wotan shouts. He must of course; for even though he is appalled at Alberich's vileness, he knows that without the ring he may as well have no power at all. Real power cannot tolerate any power beyond its control, especially of the threatening kind.

If Wotan's ideal of a self-limiting power that acts with some moral responsibility was a paradox before, it is now like a wisp of vapor vanishing forever. Wotan is already up to his throat in irre-

sponsible acts. As he tacitly agrees to Loge's proposition for get-
ting Alberich's ring, he loses moral stature. How does one get the
ring, Wotan inquires. "By theft!" Loge answers: "What a thief
stole, you steal from the thief!" It is, as Loge puts it, literally
"child's play." Fafner and Fasolt, too, are frightened. But they are
also set on obtaining the ring. Naïvely Fafner tells Wotan that
they will forego the goddess of youth and beauty for the metal.
Wotan, as we expect, once again shrewdly evades them, saying
that he cannot very well promise them something he himself does
not possess. The giants, therefore, drag away Freia, and they will
keep her unless by evening Wotan turns up with the gold. With
their assurance of youth gone, the gods rapidly begin to age.
Wotan resolves to descend immediately with Loge into the en-
trails of the earth in order, in some way, to rob Alberich of the
gold.

By his deeds Wotan has become inevitably an extension of Alberich. But Alberich is already his extension, for Wotan, after all,
has destroyed the World Ash. The Nibelung's theft is merely an
enlargement of the god's primary transgression. Thus it is not sur-
prising that Wotan must break his own laws by stealing just in
order to insure his power, in fact, his very life. Power, Wotan soon
discovers, is a horror of irresponsibility and immoral acts.

As the musicologist Edward Downes rightly points out, "the
third scene of the opera, with Alberich wielding the master's whip
and the helpless Nibelungs mining gold in the dark shafts of Ni-
belheim, is a somber, frightening picture, obviously an allegory of
the slaves of capitalism, the sweated labor, and the foul working
conditions that did exist in many a factory and mine." [7] In short, it
is Marx; but it is more than that. Wagner is now less concerned
with revolutionary change than with essential human values, with
the basic significance of the human condition itself. He sees
Alberich, who has harshly enslaved the Nibelungs and even his
own brother Mime, as the incarnation of insatiable lusts and un-
heard of cruelties. Yet Loge, through a cunning ruse, outmaneu-
vers the power-mad gnome who holds aloft the ring and proclaims
that *he* will master the whole world.

Loge then tricks Alberich into assuming the form of a tiny
creature by putting on his head the "Tarnhelm," which lends the
wearer any desired shape. As a toad, Alberich is vincible at last.
Wotan and the fire-god bind him and drag him up to their col-

leagues. Merely in order to free himself, Alberich must now order his slaves to pile up all the gold in his possession. Wotan finally demands the precious ring. Alberich screams that he would rather lay down his life; but give it he must when the god rips the ring from his finger. The dwarf's shriek of terror appropriately introduces his long curse upon the ring. He who has it will be wracked by fear and ill fortune, and he who does not have it shall be gnawed by envy and greed. This, however, is only the outward symbolization of a curse that has long been in force.

The effects of possessing the gold, now beginning to transpire, are seen to be as sordid as they are fateful. Wotan, slipping on his stolen prize, holds up his hand intoxicated by the gleaming treasure he owns for the moment. He hopes to pay the giants, who now return with Freia, with the rest of the gold. But he begins to feel disgust as he sees the degrading demand of the giants fulfilled. They have insisted that if they must do without the goddess of youth and beauty, her whole figure must be so hidden behind the pile of golden treasure that not even a glimmer of her eye or her lovely golden hair may be seen. It is very ignoble business, especially since Wotan is at last forced to relinquish the ring he has just acquired. But now, during the sordid concealment of Freia behind the heaps of gold, Wotan, even though shaken by the repulsive scene, still firmly refuses to part with the ring. Yet he is compelled to give it up, if only to fill the last remaining chink in Freia's wall of gold; through the tiny space there gleams even yet, Fasolt insists, the glistening loveliness of the maiden's eye. Nonetheless, Wotan refuses once more. At this distressing point, Erda, the goddess of wisdom, rises eerily from the earth and admonishes the stubborn god to release the ring! "All things that are," Erda reveals, "come to their end. A gloomy day breaks for the gods. Thus I advise you: give up the ring."

> Alles, was ist, endet.
> Ein düsterer Tag
> dämmert den Göttern:
> Dir rat' ich, meide den Ring!

And Wotan does precisely as he must. People in Wagner's day, however, and some people ever since, were truly perplexed by the fact that Wotan and his entire order, in view of his actually freeing himself from the accursed metal, nevertheless must eventually perish.

But in the prose sketch for *Das Rheingold*, quite unlike the final version of the text, Wagner clarifies this problem. In the sketch, both Wagner and Erda—but not Wotan—realize the impassable barrier that the god's power has reached. Wotan has, after all, by now ruined not only the World Ash, he has also resorted to treachery and crime merely in order to obtain the ring, and with it total power. He is therefore doomed from the start, so that even by the end of *Rheingold* his entire position may be viewed as simply untenable. An inescapable *Götterdämmerung* already looms blackly.

Wagner's sketch is quite explicit about all this. In it Erda informs Wotan: "The gods are in trouble if they deceive with treaties; Wotan will be in difficulty far worse if he holds on to the ring; all of them approach their end slowly, *but the end will come upon them instantly* unless they rid themselves of the ring." (*Italics mine*)[8] Death, in other words, requires sacrifices, or else it comes at once.

Yet for Wotan, and for many a Wagner student past and present, Erda's warning appears to carry no such somber prediction. It remains "mysterious," exactly as Wotan states. Wagner's second thoughts, in the final text, about allowing Erda's message to remain cryptic seem apropos: Wotan does not yet comprehend all the terrifying and devious ways of power as seen by Wagner. Nonetheless, it is patent already at this point in the vast scheme of the *Ring* how crucially Erda's pronouncement ties in with the ultimate catastrophe of the Wagnerian universe. Wotan contemptuously, and with some bitterness, throws the ring to the giants, so that Freia is able to return happily to her loved ones.

It can no longer appear cryptic, even though it still does to Wotan, that although he *does* heed Erda's warning he must perish anyway. Effectively elusive as Erda's words seem to him, Wotan is yet aware that at least he may no longer hope to pilot the world's destiny; nor can he, as he later tells the earth goddess, "hinder the rolling wheel" of the disastrous outcome. Wagner is saying that power not only may never be reconciled with order and moral responsibility, but that it shatters freedom and love as well, just as the events in *Die Walküre* demonstrate. In *Rheingold*, Wagner makes plain that the sole force that motivates and sustains power is *more* power and, if necessary, force, guile, and violence as well.

The very moment at which the giants attain it potentially with the ring's possession, power turns into a veritable horror before the eyes of all the gods. Fafner quickly and brutally pounds his more sensitive brother to death, so that he may keep the new treasure for himself. The curse of the metal has shown its potency.

In recent Bayreuth productions Richard Wagner's grandson, Wieland, made sure that Fasolt's mangled body remains on stage during the entire final scene. Even at the very end, when the gods have all but disappeared, Fasolt still lies there. This is as it should be.

Loge also remains behind, with his back to the deceptive splendor of the new Walhalla, which the gods now enter. Just as the Rhine daughters from the abyss plead with Wotan to return their gold by calling him false, Loge confidently predicts his end: "They who believe that their rule will last," he announces to himself, "merely plunge toward disaster."

II *The Horror of Parenthood*

The rainbow bridge across which the gods stride into the security of the fortress Walhalla proves to be of thin air. Like the beguiling rainbow, Walhalla itself is hardly more than a chimera. At best, it is a trap: although it appears solid and safe, it turns out to be incapable of shielding its leader against the threatening power now loose in the world in the form of Fafner's treasure; upon it the giant—transformed into a mighty serpent—now sleeps. (In the 1965 Bayreuth staging of *Das Rheingold*, the façade of the castle was indeed heavily lined with what appeared to be prison bars.)

If he could engender blind instruments of his will, Wotan reasons, who one day might be able to provide his needs for greater security and fulfill his hopes for the creation of genuine freedom —a freedom that remains denied to him because of the self-limiting laws on his own spear—then he might deflect the black tide of the Nibelungs' hate and restore the primacy of his world order. Accordingly, Wotan becomes a parent. He first sires with Erda nine Valkyrie daughters, whose leader is Brünnhilde, and then fathers, with a woman unnamed, the twins Siegmund and Sieglinde. If Brünnhilde is to be exploited in one way, then the twins, as a loving pair, can be exploited less directly in another. Brünnhilde and her sisters, Wotan believes, are to be abject instruments of his will and shall "choose the slain" from the battlefield to bolster Walhalla's endangered defenses, whereas Siegmund, who shall hopefully find and wield his father's sword—the symbolic significance is clear—is to bring about that "free deed" which, paradoxically, is forbidden "the god."

Each one of Wotan's apparently conflicting needs merely reflects the various ways in which parental authority seeks the exploitation of offspring as blind instruments of its will. Nor is this all. For as soon as the offspring rip away the masks of the sanctity of parenthood, the parent casts them off and even cuts them down as no longer serviceable tools of his divinity. Seldom in drama has the nature of parenthood, with its intrinsic horrors, been as neatly exposed as Wagner does throughout the *Ring*.

While Brünnhilde and her sisters in battle gallop the slaughtered heroes up to Wotan to defend his shaky rule, Siegmund performs his supposedly "free" act when he pulls the sword from the ash tree into which the god had once thrust it and left it for him. He then abducts his willing twin Sieglinde from her legal master Hunding, and unites himself with her. It is the pivot of Wotan's grand idea that the wedded siblings are to produce the fearless and world-delivering Siegfried. Thus, Siegmund's sword—the god believes—is the answer to his own spear. In this, however, Wotan has succumbed to a monstrous illusion. For as the omnipotent parent he is soon forced to shatter the sword in his son's very hands; yet in the hands of Siegfried that same sword one day will smash the spear. Wotan, indeed, is rapidly compelled to realize that he has set his own trap. In Act Two of *Die Walküre*, under the pressure of Fricka's just arguments, the quicksand under the god's whole notion of himself and his plans is relentlessly exposed.

Wotan's spouse, first of all, demands irately that Siegmund should be punished. He has broken not only her marriage laws by abducting Sieglinde from her husband, but in addition, his bond with her is incestuous. Wotan attempts, at first, to employ his illusions about freedom in order to protect Siegmund's embarrassing but—to Wotan—justifiable deeds. Uncorrupted by his father's power, unfettered by the laws of the spear and without its protection, Siegmund quickly discovers, and will use, his father's sword. However, Fricka now points out that Siegmund's father is the victim of a huge deception, a basic paradox. Whoever knew of gods, Fricka asks, who create heroes to perform what they themselves could not do?

The holes in Wotan's armor are laid bare here for the second time, as they initially were in *Das Rheingold* when Fasolt accused Wotan of duplicity and revealed that all of his power rests solely on the laws and treaties of his spear. Fricka now ponders how a slave is to turn into a free individual when, in fact, free men have virtually become slaves. At this important juncture, the prose sketch makes once more apparent what the final text, with its alliteration and poetic syntax, does not. In the sketch, Fricka tells Wotan that Siegmund defies the law only because of the god's approval and protection. Wagner's marginal notation, moreover, expresses his real intentions in this matter even more unmistakably. This marginal addition is placed directly opposite Fricka's remark about Wotan's protection of Siegmund. It affirms "Fricka's contempt for the heroes, who in themselves are absolutely nothing, but who, instead, derive their entire existence through Wotan alone." [9] Siegmund's free will is nothing but the god's projection, and the "need" of which Wotan speaks, together with the delivering sword, is a deception.

Wotan has been broken. Now, and for the first time, he sees that whereas Fricka has been telling him that he is deceiving *her*, he has in fact been deceiving himself. He suddenly knows that his order and its laws not only cannot create freedom; they cannot even guarantee it while it exists. He is prevented from creating freedom simply because it would be a direct contradiction of the power he must enforce. Not only Siegmund's freedom, but his love union with Sieglinde is doomed. Wotan's novel insight into the exigencies of his power, irrespective of Fricka's threats, makes him helpless when she demands his promise to avenge the transgressed marriage laws. Siegmund must be slain in the coming fight with Hunding, the avenging spouse. Siegmund's "invincible" sword is to be made powerless also; and Fricka demands that even Brünnhilde, who is Wotan's favorite and chief among the Valkyries, be prevented from shielding Siegmund in combat. For who is Brünnhilde except a part of the god's own will?

Wotan's despair is total. He realizes that he is helpless to alter the nature of power, be it that of the parent or the upholder of social order. He now admits to Brünnhilde what Fasolt and Fricka have told him: "How cunningly I wished to lie to myself; so easily Fricka unmasked my own fraud and delusion!" Wotan orders his daughter to destroy Siegmund's freedom and, in effect, his very life. Brünnhilde is repelled. Not even at this stage does she comprehend the nature of her father's paradox, *i.e.*, why he must kill what he loves the most. Stern and frustrated, Wotan forces his daughter's submission to parental authority. "Siegmund falls!" the god shouts in a wrathful cloud as he storms away. Wotan himself has reached the end; he has learned to *will* his utter annihilation. It remains for Wagner to show why he has no choice but to destroy his favorite child, too, when she rebels at being his instrument of divine authority.

Brünnhilde attempts to shield Siegmund in his combat with Hunding. Out of genuine empathy for Siegmund's plight and his love for Sieglinde, the Valkyrie disobeys her father. For this, Wotan plans to crush her with a fury. Having appeared at the combat and seen to it that Siegmund is smashed, his sword—Wotan's "idea"—left shattered, the god charges after his daughter to find her hiding amid her Valkyrie sisters. Fleeing to them, she bore the horrified Sieglinde on her steed, together with the splintered sword. Now, before Wotan arrives, Brünnhilde reveals to Sieglinde that she carries Siegmund's child. Siegfried, interpreted by Wagner as "the bringer of peace through victory," is to be his name. With the sword's fragments Sieglinde is to be concealed in the forest so that she may give birth to the hero.

Wotan's anger, when he comes upon the Valkyries, is immense simply from the awareness that his beloved daughter has dared to carry out what he himself could never have done because of his own laws. But he joyfully would have liked to have done it, and this irony sparks the storm within him. Brünnhilde's punishment, therefore, is to become what, in fact, she now is: no longer a Valkyrie and no more her father's treasured offspring, the happy yet inextricable part of his will. She is never to see him again; instead she must be put to sleep unguarded in the open, the helpless booty of any male who might wish to make her his menial wife. With her divinity taken away, she is to be a slave. She must be totally cast out, because Wotan has no choice.

Actually Brünnhilde has cast herself out of the parental heaven before Wotan informs her of her "punishment." She did this at the moment when she sought to resolve the schism that she knew was tearing Wotan apart. In "sharing Siegmund's victory or his death," as she realized she must, she felt that she was also demonstrating empathy for her father's predicament. Yet at this point, having matured very quickly, Brünnhilde grows wise. She gains insight into the horror of Wotan's power, as soon as she perceives that the very empathy that tried to preserve *him* and Siegmund must be destroyed by the moral irresponsibility stemming from his inner division (*Zwiespalt*). What is more, Brünnhilde now pierces the illusion of the divinity of parenthood. She sees the horror of the deceptive parental love which seeks to exploit the offspring as an instrument of the will and, if unsuccessful, to crush it.

In essence, then, Wotan takes Brünnhilde's godhead away because she has already taken it away from him. Brünnhilde knows that if Wotan's power and parental will destroy freedom, they also destroy love. Following Fasolt and Fricka, the god's own daughter now becomes the third person to expose Wotan to the scrutiny of his tragic and impossible condition, when she tells him: "When Fricka made you estranged to your own plan by forcing you to follow hers, you became your own enemy."

At the end, however, Brünnhilde endeavors to soften Wotan's sentence. She tells him that he really would not wish to dishonor the eternal part of himself, "to cut away your own half that once belonged to you wholly." She pleads with her father to encircle her sleeping place with terrifying curtains of fire, so that only the bravest man may hope to penetrate the flames to win her. She speaks to Wotan more as a partner than as a child: She is thinking about Siegfried, the hope of Sieglinde's womb. Wotan too thinks of this second experiment in "free" heroes. Then he tenderly erases his child's godhead and her consciousness with a long kiss upon her eyelids. After laying Brünnhilde down for years of slumber, Wotan commands Loge to gird her rocky height with a sea of fire in words that are a devastating comment on the nature of his power: "Let the bride be freed by one who is freer than I—the god!" Wotan in fact still hopes that he can create freedom somehow, *in spite of* himself and all the authority of his divine establishment. He remains optimistic enough to believe, at the end of *Die Walküre*, that Siegfried may yet be able to bring it about.

However, in the Nibelung dwarf Mime, who is Alberich's brother, Siegfried inherits the same kind of parental authority that destroyed his father. Yet Mime-Siegfried is merely a grotesque travesty of the type of relationship that exists between Wotan and Brünnhilde, and between him and Siegmund. But the basic parent-child relationship, as Wagner had exposed it earlier, is still there. First we see Mime attempting to coerce Siegfried's filial affection by detailing numerous examples—and always cleverly sung to the same repetitious musical phrase—of "look at all the nice things I've already done for you." When these props of parental authority fail, Mime tries to frighten the boy into feeling the impact of fear, which Siegfried refuses to become aware of. By such means Mime hopes to dupe the youngster into serving as an instrument of his will and his evil plans. When even this does not work properly, the dwarf, in Act Two of *Siegfried*, seeks to kill the hero and would have done so if the young man had not learned of his purpose and destroyed Mime first.

Before Siegfried was born, Mime nursed Sieglinde in her pregnancy. She gave him the pieces of the sword for his trouble. Then she died. When we first see her son at the opening of *Siegfried*, he has turned into a strong teen-ager who despises the sinister and ugly dwarf who, he realizes, could scarcely pretend to be his true parent. Siegfried is thoroughly sick, moreover, of watching this fatherly monster laboring to weld and hammer together the two pieces of Siegmund's weapon. Taking the fragments into his own hands, the son forges the invincible sword.

Mime would be terrorized were it not for his plan of doing the boy in as soon as he carries through his task: to slay the serpent Fafner and thereby, once more, free the whole golden treasure, including the omnipotent ring and "Tarnhelm," on which the dragon has been sleeping ever since the end of *Das Rheingold*. Yet Alberich, too, yearns for these tools of world power. As Wotan does in his guise of a Wanderer, Alberich now observes events from the side. But whereas Wotan is sure that his grandson will produce a better world once he has slain Fafner and obtained the ring, Mime's brother hopes that the boy and Fafner will kill each other. He is, however, more seriously hopeful that Siegfried, rather than Mime, will get the ring, simply because Siegfried, unlike his own brother, is completely unaware of its power and would never enslave him, as his brother would surely do.

After Siegfried has stabbed the dragon to death and raised his blood-stained fingers to his lips, he understands the language of the forest bird, who warns him of Mime's treacherous aims. He promptly strikes Mime down, and the hidden Alberich accompanies his brother's death with triumphant, mocking laughter. Siegfried, indeed, admits that he is fearless; for even in the bloody combat with Fafner he did not learn the meaning of fear. He also remains unwitting of the power of the ring he now wears and of the "Tarnhelm." The forest bird describes Brünnhilde's sleeping place and advises Siegfried that since he is fearless he may reach the maiden, who will then be his. The bird will lead him there.

Although the stupid youngster—Wagner makes no attempt to hide the fact—has already done away with the horror of one parent, he must yet confront another. Wotan himself firmly blocks the path to his daughter's fiery bed, but Siegfried is driven to smite the last vestige of fatherly authority and, at the same time, the Wanderer's final pretension to power.

Before the catastrophic blow, however, the fading god stakes his destiny on Erda's counsel. In night and storm he raises the deity from wisdom's sleep. Realizing that his whole world is about to crash, Wotan asks the goddess of all knowledge "how to brake a rolling wheel?" Erda's impatience with the old man's questions, her downright indifference to his perplexity, burst into genuine irritation as soon as she learns how Brünnhilde has fared at his hands: "Doing penance in bonds of sleep while her mother of wisdom slept." Following Fasolt in *Das Rheingold,* as well as the subsequent revelations of Fricka and Brünnhilde, Erda angrily exposes the horror of Wotan's power, as she has just revealed the horror of his parenthood, by flinging the facts straight into his teeth.

"Since when," she inquires, "does he who teaches stubbornness and defiance punish it and grow furious at a deed he himself ignited?" How does it come about, she continues, that "the one upholding laws and just agreements prevents justice and rules through lies?" Her tirade ends in a vehement outburst: "You are not what you believe you are!" Thus Erda confirms Wotan's inevitable *Götterdämmerung* that loomed as soon as he laid waste the World Ash. The long line of the ring's circle is nearly closed.

"You are *not* what you imagine!" Wotan pounces back. "Your knowledge blows away before my will. Do you know what Wotan *wills?*" he shouts as the goddess begins to sink. Now, he proceeds, the earth mother shall sleep forever without care. And the end of the gods brings him no fear; he wills that too. A young hero can free a whole world from Alberich's curse, since he is *without fear*. Furthermore, as she begins to vanish, he proclaims to Erda: "Once awake the child of your wisdom will work world-redeeming deeds!"

With that, Wotan has shed the last of his illusions, though he does not know it. But Wagner does. Through Wagner's eyes, we can view Wotan's search for complete freedom much the same as we view Ibsen's Peer Gynt, who peels off layer after layer of the onion merely to find absolutely nothing at the core. The god's search for certain value and freedom proves that they are illusions. They cannot even be created by all of Wotan's powers. The idea of freedom and value being fashioned by power is, as Wagner shows, a basic contradiction. They cannot, Wagner seems to imply, be *created* at all.

Wotan's—and Wagner's—frustration in the face of such a fact is expressed more convincingly than anywhere in the *Ring* in the prose sketch of *Die Walküre*, Act Two, where Wotan tells his daughter: "All mankind hangs in the net of our law; they do solely what we decide shall be; their actions are carried out by our bidding alone. . . . If I could squeeze all divinity into one drop of human seed out of which one free mortal might spring, then I should destroy divinity." [10] Such has been Wotan's central idea of freedom. It provides the *Ring* with substantial ethical ballast, but hardly enough to see it through. For what was not destroyed by power is now destroyed by love. Yet as Erda vanishes, Wotan still believes in illusions of freedom that lie in the invisible heart of the metaphorical onion, in the promise of the fearless Siegfried and the redeeming deed of the awakened Brünnhilde. But the terrifying problem of how to create freedom and social justice remains unsolved.

As it turns out, Siegfried, strongly annoyed by how an old man blocks his way to the sleeping maid behind the flames, hacks the spear that rules the world as if in reply to the way the same spear shattered his father's sword. Believing only that he has thereby removed the obstacle in Brünnhilde's path, Siegfried has unwittingly signalled the annihilation of Wotan and his world.

The remainder of *Siegfried* is the history of how the young hero sees the sleeping woman and is nearly paralyzed by fear, before he is overcome by passion. Brünnhilde, in turn, is shorn of wisdom by passion for her awakener: if she redeems the world, it is only by implementing its annihilation, and her own. But first she destroys Siegfried.

CHAPTER 4

The Redemption from Love

I *Siegfried and Tristan*

EVER more persistently during the year 1857, a fresh vision intruded into Wagner's *Ring* mood. By the summer it had succeeded in interrupting not only the completion of *Siegfried* but had postponed the *Ring's* progress as well for another twelve years. The novel vision was *Tristan und Isolde*, whose seven opening notes—although Wagner did not know it then—were to transform the art of music.

With some self-discipline Wagner finished the composition of *Siegfried* as far as the end of Act Two. Almost immediately thereafter, in the course of August and September, the entire *Tristan* poem was well rounded out, beckoning his Muse to flood it with life. Bursting from his pen under intense pressure over the next two years, first in Zurich, then in Venice, and finally in Lucerne, *Tristan und Isolde* was completed by August, 1859. Reading through the entire score a year later, Wagner expressed to Mathilde Wesendonk his astonishment over it, a sentiment with which we can still agree. "This Tristan," he wrote, "is a wonder to me! How I was able to do such a thing seems to me more and more incomprehensible: as I went through it once again, I had to tear my ears and eyes wide open!" [1]

As was usually the case in judgments involving his own work, Wagner was right. This volcano of a score proved indeed to contain the most unique and influential sounds to erupt in Wagner's century. *Tristan* was revolution. The harmonic progressions of its initial theme alone—its acoustic idea—questioned and eroded the very ground of a musical tradition of centuries, and scattered the flow of tonality, perhaps forever, from its long, deep bed. Much of the serious music we today call "modern" virtually has its roots here.

Yet the reasons that Wagner gave to friends for his radical shift of plans during the summer of 1857 are astounding for their naïve optimism, particularly in the light of the subsequently revealed facts. He claimed, first of all, that he desired to bring forth a more "practical" work for the stage than the mammoth *Ring*, whose unprecedented length and scenic demands would, he judged correctly, prove very hazardous for the theaters of his day. The comparatively modest project he now had in mind, he insisted, would certainly be within the scope and ken of ordinary stages. He even felt that the new work was so undemanding that for a time he seriously pondered the prospect of a première *in Italian* to be given at Rio de Janeiro, at the invitation of the Emperor of Brazil, Dom Pedro II.

How truly sanguine Wagner's hopes were, was shown, however, when *Tristan und Isolde* was shelved by the theater in Karlsruhe as being simply incapable of being performed; and later, during the early 1860's, it was dropped by Vienna's most competent opera because of vocal difficulties. A Berlin journalist ably depicts the whole situation in Karlsruhe at that time: "Ostensibly the shelving of the work was on the singers' account; but according to trustworthy reports, the demands made on the orchestra are equally exorbitant and impossible to meet." [2] Wagner's incorrigible optimism remained unvindicated until June, 1865, when in Munich *Tristan* was at last brought to life by all the authority and financial resources of Wagner's youthful rescuer, the recently enthroned King Ludwig II of Bavaria.

What was the reason for Wagner's laying *Siegfried* aside at that particular point? Actually, he did not lay it aside. That he reached an impasse in the *Ring*—near the point where he knew he must conceive musically that crucial confrontation between Siegfried and Brünnhilde, when his fearlessness and her wisdom were both to be destroyed by love—had its cause in reasons that were, he soon realized, a reflection of profound inner changes rather than the superficial reasons he gave to his friends and, in the beginning, to himself. Yet even Ernest Newman, Wagner's most authoritative biographer, writes, without further comment, that, "perhaps the profoundest reason of all for his abandoning the *Ring* lay in his subconscious." [3] Newman is probably correct. Now, however, we realize that in the process of working out *Tristan* within himself Wagner was not actually putting what remained of *Sieg-*

fried out of his thoughts at all; nor, for that matter, the important consideration of how his tetralogy might be concluded. That is to say, before he could complete *Siegfried*, and endure to dwell on how he wanted his *Ring* really to end—it perplexed him for years —Wagner felt compelled to round out and virtually solve the problem of *Siegfried* by creating first a *Tristan und Isolde*. It meant solving the major problem of the adequacy of passion and transcendental love. Far from merely being shunted aside, then, *Siegfried* was looked upon somewhat as the bone and blood to *Tristan*'s sinew and skin. Let us see why this is so.

The all-important link between the two works, revealing *Tristan* as the result of the disturbing insights gained in confronting the problematical nature of erotic love at the end of *Siegfried*, begins to reach light in a letter of August 23, 1856. Wagner writes to August Röckel about the difficulties he is having with the words of Brünnhilde that are to conclude the *Ring*. He has discovered—so he tells his friend—that Brünnhilde's message about love as the sole source of salvation, a love that is to prevail in the world in place of mendacious laws and treaties, and to supplant greed for wealth and power, is, in fact, "biased and tendentious." Moreover, Wagner states that these lines regarding love had been conceived at a time when, he says, he "was scarcely clear in my mind (unfortunately!) what kind of love I was actually talking of, a love that, in the course of the myth, we indeed beheld as being absolutely destructive." [4] As a consequence of these new insights, Brünnhilde's concluding phrase in *Die Götterdämmerung* about "love being blessed in pleasure and grief," is now transformed into what amounts to a complete antithesis. Now Brünnhilde ends the *Ring* with a speech about a love that has brought her such enormous grief that her "eyes were opened" and she beheld the end of the world. Accordingly, it is as significant as it is unsurprising when Wagner, near the conclusion of this same letter, mentions that "besides the Nibelungen pieces I have yet a *Tristan and Isolde* (love as a terrible torment) in my head." [5]

By August, 1856, then, Wagner already had come to regard the love between Siegfried and Brünnhilde as exceedingly equivocal; and this new perception, from the important evidence just given, quite obviously awakened and catalyzed a fresh vision of Tristan's and Isolde's passion as "love as a terrible torment" (*die Liebe als furchtbare Qual*). Wagner's candid elucidations on the subject of

erotic love precisely at this time, and at this point in the *Ring*,
make it unquestionably clear why, during the following year, he
had to interrupt *Siegfried* so that he could first confront and work
out the whole problem of transcendental "romance" in *Tristan
und Isolde*. Wagner, in other words, had to discover at first hand
why love, as he knew it was to develop in Act Three of *Siegfried*
and in *Die Götterdämmerung*, proved to be "so absolutely destructive."

The charming tale, current and beloved now for generations, of
Mathilde Wesendonk's being the "inspiration" for Wagner's "great
love drama" is, alas, but a colorful absurdity. That intelligent and
attractive woman, who by 1857 had been happily married for nine
years and was the mother of three children, brought the oversensi-
tive composer much of the empathy and appreciation that were
usually beyond the willingness, or capacity, of Minna. Mathilde
and her husband Otto, moreover, not only helped to fill Wagner's
often bottomless purse, but also quartered him and Minna, during
much of 1857 and 1858, in a pleasant cottage, the Asyl, in back of
their own proud villa overlooking Lake Zurich.

If Mathilde was the inspiration for anything, it was the first act
of *Die Walküre*, composed in 1854; in its score there are at least
sixteen references to her in the form of initials standing cryptically
for Wagner's own phrases of affection, but which significantly
punctuate as well the mounting passion between Siegmund and
Sieglinde. It is quite patent that here, in any case, Mathilde sup-
plied the composer with a definite emotional stance, of the kind
he apparently required in order more expressively to conceive in
musical terms the love of his twins. Whatever emotional thrust
she might have contributed to the *Tristan* score, however, is far
less certain. Wagner's famous letters to her from Venice hardly
reveal any such state of affairs.

But if Mathilde's influence on the "eroticism" of *Tristan* could
be anywhere detected, it ought to be recorded in those Venetian
messages. For it was in Venice, during the latter part of 1858 and
the first quarter of 1859, that Wagner was bringing into the world
the broiling second act of *Tristan*. This is not the case, however.
The work's incandescence is scarcely reflected in these letters,
which deal, instead, with elucidations of the most cerebral sort on
compassion and empathy, involving humans and animals alike,
and with philosophical plans concerning a new work—*Parsifal*—

which yet lay far in the future. These letters, then, if they help us to comprehend anything about Wagner, permit us to glean why he was creating a *Tristan und Isolde* at all. His reasons had precious little to do with Mathilde Wesendonk.

We may state, then, that what Wagner had conceived merely in symbolic terms in the Siegfried-Brünnhilde scene, whose final textual form dates from 1852, could now be fathomed *conceptually* only by the working out of *Tristan*. Now we discover exactly what we expect: that the key metaphor representing love in Act Three of *Siegfried*, the alliterative phrase *die wonnig wogende Welle* ("the rapturous, surging wave"), becomes the dominant symbolic image pervading the transcendent vision of the lovers. And this is precisely as it should be, for the rapturous and turbulent "wave" that engulfs Brünnhilde at the conclusion of *Siegfried* becomes for Isolde the all-consuming element in which her very existence is drowned. We need not wonder whether Wagner perceived the rightness of deliberately employing this wave metaphor. It is more than clear that he did, and that he was conceiving in intellectual terms what had been actually expressed only symbolically in the *Siegfried* poem five years earlier. Therefore it will be imperative to follow Wagner's own chronology by starting with the final scene of *Siegfried*.

Having penetrated the fires that gird Brünnhilde's place of slumber, Siegfried learns all the fear and anguish of erotic desire when he cuts through the sleeping figure's armor with his sword and glimpses her womanly shape. Spying suddenly the true image that lies behind the object of his torment, Siegfried cries for his mother to help him. Freud was to say no more.

Awakening Brünnhilde with a long kiss, the boy soon overwhelms her with descriptions of his yearning. But Brünnhilde, joyfully opening her eyes on the sunny world and realizing who the awakener really is, becomes terrified. She fears that were she to surrender to his ardent feelings—and her own—both their identities would be smothered in passion. She tells Siegfried how she has looked forward to the day that has come now, for it is the day that she hopes will see Wotan's great "thought" come to life. Brünnhilde informs the impetuous youngster that she loves him out of complete empathy: "What you do not know, I will know *for* you; yet my knowing comes only by loving you." Indeed, Wotan's great "thought" was for Brünnhilde simply her profound love for the free Siegfried. But Siegfried, unfortunately, has not the smallest inkling of what she is talking about, even though he exclaims that what she tells him *sounds* lovely. So Brünnhilde, at the last, is inspired to teach him love not out of passion, but solely on the foundation of knowledge and empathy. All the poetry of her instruction makes it no less apt and graphic.

Brünnhilde describes to Siegfried how the surface of a brook is like an unbroken, perfect mirror. He rejoiced once, she tells him, on seeing his own image clearly reflected in the water. But Brünnhilde warns him that if he were to distort the brook's glassy surface into "waves," if the water's clear mirror were to be broken into inconstant ripples by his hand, he would see himself no longer. She cautions Siegfried, therefore, to seek and love only his own clear image, to attain but his own free identity. Yet all of Brünnhilde's lucid imagery leaves Siegfried as uncomprehending and passionate as before. "Love—yourself," the maiden warns, "and leave me: destroy not what is your own!"

Siegfried, however, is wildly impatient. He is only able to liken his emotions—significantly indeed—to Brünnhilde's ecstatically churning "wave," that same wave, he confesses happily, that will shatter the image of himself. Rather than calmly viewing his own image in the brook, Siegfried claims that he is eager to dive and splash into that clear surface which Brünnhilde has just shown him. Only then, he proclaims, can he cool down the yearning flames and drown his lust in the watery torrent. With a single plunge, Siegfried seeks to destroy not only his own clear image; he also yearns to drag Brünnhilde down into the foaming abyss.

Brünnhilde, who is gradually aware that this fate is the punishing rod under Wotan's fatherly glove, soon describes her surrender to passion, her own being overcome by *die wonnig wogende Welle*. Beneath the novel impact of eroticism, she finds herself unable to withstand, let alone reverse, the engulfing tide of "the rapturous, surging wave." She now admits that she must "love" Siegfried at last, but not without envisioning also their destruction through love. The important words with which they bring this scene to an end are *"leuchtende Liebe, lachender Tod!"* (gleaming love, laughing death). What Wagner means by this is that "death" is the consequence of "love"; actually, they turn out to be equivalent. It is precisely this irony which Wagner felt he must expose and finally resolve in *Tristan und Isolde* before he could proceed to that scene which he knew to be absolutely crucial for the entire development of the *Ring*. It is fully apparent now why Wagner, once he had gathered keen insight into the meaning of Siegfried's "rapturous, surging wave," was actually forced to drastically reconceive Brünnhilde's closing words about love in *Die Götterdämmerung*, words that signify not a redemption *through* love, but *from* it. This new conception also makes it entirely clear why, in the course of 1857, Wagner was driven to spell out so carefully the whole problem in a new work.

Characteristically, the Tristan problem—that of erotic love—had by then solved itself. This is evident from the fact that the final text of *Tristan und Isolde* was set down in a matter of just three weeks during August and September of that year. In it, the metaphysical dream of all lovers, their transcendent vision of love as a realm of everlasting and supreme value, is subjected to the most thoroughgoing scrutiny, and with the expected result. The transcendental vision of the lovers becomes unmasked for what it really is: emotional quicksand, a deceiving and destructive "wave," whose illusion eventually submerges their identities and engulfs their lives, exactly as we see happen in the instance of Siegfried and Brünnhilde. Let us see how this comes about.

II Tristan und Isolde

The pair fall in love in Ireland, where Tristan had slain Isolde's uncle Morold, who was Ireland's king. As Isolde was helping Tristan's wound to heal, the two became aware of their profound attachment. Yet Tristan must bring the Irish maiden, untouched and under guard, as bride to his lord, the elderly King Mark of Cornwall. The couple on board ship are held apart by Tristan's code of knightly honor and Isolde's sense of deep disgrace. Isolde decides to bridge the abyss of frustration extending between them by commanding her servant Brangäne to prepare a potion of death. When Tristan is offered the fatal brew by Isolde's own hand as a "drink of reconciliation," the knight knows better. What, at least in theatrical terms, they do not know as they hasten to empty the cup, is that they have each been cheated by Brangäne, who has carefully substituted for the potion of death (*Todestrank*) a love potion (*Liebestrank*). Once they have drunk it down, every barrier that formerly might have held them apart is instantly and disastrously torn down. Their passionate yearning for each other has now reached a point beyond any possibility of relief. They henceforth subsist solely on the notion of their love as a supreme and omnipotent value.

As their ship drops anchor in Cornwall and King Mark himself enters the vessel to greet them, Tristan no longer knows what king he is and Isolde asks desperately if indeed she must continue living. But what captures our attention most is the way in which the lovers have just expressed their new and complete isolation from the world. They describe it precisely in the terms we expect, the "rapturous, surging wave" metaphor of *Siegfried:* "How our hearts surgingly rise! How all our senses rapturously tremble!" (*Wie sich die Herzen wogend erheben! Wie alle Sinne wonnig erbeben!*)

The rapturous waves in the nocturnal fountain, which Isolde describes at the beginning of the next act as she awaits Tristan, consistently carry through Wagner's effective imagery. In the long colloquy of the lovers that follows, Wagner elaborately works out the means whereby Tristan and Isolde are to become "night-sighted" (*nachtsichtig*); how they are to attain a transcendental oneness in night and death that will obliterate the mortal individuality forced on them by the sunlit reality of "the day," which they despise.

Wagner allows Tristan and Isolde painfully to seek out by themselves a way for their union to survive immortally. They discover, however, that such an everlasting union would signify the total loss of their identities, simply because what Isolde calls "this lovely little word: *and*" that links them so tenuously would, she points out, be obliterated by their deaths. But Tristan's vision remains as yet less questioning. He implies that in reality identity merely disturbs their ideal of perfect value by hindering its pure fulfillment. Only death, therefore, would remove the one barrier that prevents Tristan from loving Isolde eternally. But "this little word: *and*" that binds their love, how else could it be destroyed, Isolde continues to ask, except by Isolde's very life if death came to Tristan?

They ultimately realize, of course, that only their total dissolution, the end of all mortal identity in death, will at last bring about a union that is as complete as it is perpetual. A union of this kind, however, can be nothing but a complete illusion, for reality must always intervene, as Tristan discovers before Isolde at last returns to him near the very end. No sooner does Isolde arrive to greet him when Tristan, with her name on his lips, dies of the "wound" given him by Melot when he surprised the lovers in Act Two.

Tristan dies, but not without first having penetrated his great illusion with a bracing insight. He now understands that it was he alone who brewed all the poison in the *Liebestrank*. It can no longer appear as a coincidence that the *Liebestrank* was once substituted for the *Todestrank* by Isolde's well-meaning servant Brangäne. This very substitution, however, really expresses the same love-death equivocation as the "*leuchtende Liebe, lachender Tod*" symbolism at the conclusion of *Siegfried*. But with a certain difference. Now Wagner cannot have the slightest doubt as to why transcendental love is "absolutely destructive." He has discovered with Siegfried and Brünnhilde just what he had discovered with Tristan and Isolde, namely, that "love" is a complete violation of their personalities; he has now found out why lovers deny each other the right of personality. That is to say, Wagner shows us why lovers do not choose to regard or affirm each other's identity at all; they seek rather to destroy, or at least suppress, each other's freedom, solely in order that their notion of transcendent love may survive.

In *Beyond the Tragic Vision*, Morse Peckham argues that *Tristan* is an exploration of the significance of *Siegfried*'s last scene. He is absolutely right when he states that erotic love, as Wagner shows it operating in both works, is "a projection, a self-created mask which the lover places over the face and the form of the beloved. Lovers do not see each other at all. They see only themselves." Peckham is also correct in pointing out how the long duet between Tristan and Isolde in Act Two "is entirely an analysis of how two lovers exploit each other's emotions." [6]

Similarly, one lover cannot actually be the cause of the other's torment. Such torment can be only self-created, just as the mask itself is created for the beloved. Wagner has Tristan himself say this. In Act Three, dying of a "wound" that is really a metaphor for self-inflicted anguish, Tristan exclaims that he alone is to blame for the drink which brought him *die Liebe als furchtbare Qual*, love as a terrifying torment:

Den furchtbaren Trank,
der der Qual mich vertraut,
ich selbst, ich selbst—
ich hab' ihn gebraut!

After saying that he himself brewed all the poison of his affliction, Tristan collapses. His faithful servant Kurvenal then bends over him and, sighing, wonders what will now happen to "the world's loveliest illusion." Wagner has carefully unmasked the cherished illusion of erotic romance; but he has yet to reveal it as insanity. For, in the end, Tristan and Isolde do enter their longed-for realm of bliss—but not together. This is exactly the point. The important paradox inherent in that fact becomes explicit when Isolde, after Tristan has already been dead for some time, rises, trance-like, above his lifeless body and tries to convey to those around her how she is being engulfed by tides of the rapturous, churning wave. As she asks herself whether "they are waves of soft currents" or "swells of rapturous scents," Wagner deliberately employs the vocabulary of Siegfried's *die wonnig wogende Welle*:

. . . sind es *Wellen*
sanfter Lüfte?
Sind es *Wogen*
wonniger Düfte? (*italics mine*)

There can be no question that Wagner here consciously seeks out, once again, the wave image of *Siegfried*'s final scene, in order more graphically to depict Isolde's self-destruction through love. Tristan, too, has destroyed himself, but without Isolde. Just before she arrives, to "heal" his "wound," he rips off his bandages in ecstasy and rejoices watching the torrent of blood drain the life out of his body. Now, without Tristan, as Isolde's identity is swept away in the turbulent waters of her vision, she asks those about her if they cannot see and hear her beloved. They do not, of course, nor does she—at least not in actuality. She merely perceives her self-created projection of Tristan and dies; just as he has died seeing only his projection of her. That is why, at the very last, Wagner causes Isolde to say something that seems totally irrational, but which perfectly expresses the whole irony of her dilemma, that "to drown, to submerge oblivious, is the highest bliss!"

The utmost gratification of love's illusion, Wagner maintains, is utter oblivion, or, as Peckham says with regard to the irony of the lovers' fate, "when you are dead you can scarcely enjoy the loss of identity." [7] Wagner, it is apparent, would really prefer us *not* to participate in this consummation of Isolde's great illusion; instead, we are to penetrate it and understand it just the way Tristan does in his passage above, and then share his—and Wagner's—keen insight into the real nature of the illusion by beholding the irony of Isolde's and Tristan's fate: that the only redemption from love is death. [8]

Because of the long established Western tradition of sanctifying sexuality in romantic love, *Tristan und Isolde* has been, and remains, the least understood of Wagner's works. Far from being the grand apotheosis of erotic love for which it has, almost unanimously, been taken, the work reveals transcendental romance as being precisely what Freud later said it was: a model psychosis. Not only does love destroy reality and identity; it cannot, as Wagner shows, redeem anyone, simply because it cannot function as a genuine basis for empathy between human beings, not to mention society as a whole.

When Wagner finally took up the *Ring* again, when he could bear to go on writing it, he was wholly persuaded that the "love" between Siegfried and Brünnhilde was indeed a thoroughly destructive force.

II Die Götterdämmerung

Before completing the full score of the third act of *Siegfried* in February, 1871, Wagner worked on *Die Götterdämmerung,* whose composition, and thus that of *Der Ring des Nibelungen* as a whole, was finished, at last, on November 21, 1874. [9] Begun in September, 1853, the *Ring* had been a generation in the making. The final years of its completion saw Wagner's move from Triebschen, his home near Lucerne, Switzerland, to Bayreuth, the sleepy town in northern Bavaria that soon was to be a word synonymous with his own name. Shortly after bringing the *Ring* to a close, the Festival Theater that since then has practically institutionalized him was completed, with Ludwig II's help, on the hill north of the town. There, during August, 1876, three complete *Ring* cycles were first performed for the general public and numerous crowned heads of Europe, who considered it their duty to attend, thus attesting to the reputation Wagner had by then achieved. But they understood no more of what Wagner was talking about in the *Ring* than most people do today.

In the final part of the tetralogy, Alberich, through his bastard son Hagen, still contemplates total domination of the world by means of the ring. But at this stage in Wagner's master plan, the capture of the cursed gold had become little more than the necessary implementation of a long familiar plot. Nor do Wotan and his gods make up the true substance of events. Power, we recall, has long been out of Wotan's hands; it was utterly and irretrievably smashed by Siegfried's sword. Wotan's final act of power is merely to command the complete demolition of the World Ash which he had once mutilated. The mighty splendor of its faraway past is now to serve Wotan only as logs heaped about the walls of Walhalla, to help burn it to ashes in the last conflagration. Sitting with his gods and the chosen slain in his lofty hall, Wotan himself regally awaits the flaming catastrophe at the end of the world, just as the Norns have predicted.

The real substance of *Die Götterdämmerung* is filled up by the "absolutely destructive" hate-love of Brünnhilde. By having shown how Siegfried destroyed her wisdom and his own freedom and identity, and by revealing how Brünnhilde destroys Siegfried's life, Wagner is simply demonstrating the exercise of power on an entirely human level.

That the ring itself turns into a love token makes this even more emphatic. Up till now, it has symbolized total power to rule the world. In the Prologue of *Die Götterdämmerung*, however, it begins to operate as power on a strictly personal plane at the moment when Brünnhilde receives it as a "pledge of love" from Siegfried. In return for the ring she gives him her horse, Grane, upon which the hero rides off to his doom at Gunther's court.

Although she laments that her lover still remains "untaught," Brünnhilde herself is now shorn of wisdom by passion. For that reason she adamantly insists on keeping Siegfried's token of love even when Waltraute, her Valkyrie sister, gallops to the mountain fastness to see if she can regain it. Waltraute warns her that if the ring is not returned to the Rhine, where it always belonged, Walhalla and Wotan will surely perish. At this juncture, Brünnhilde—quite understandably—could not care less. Yet she does start to care as soon as her beloved climbs up again to the height on which he once awakened her, this time to forcefully claim her as bride for someone else. Siegfried's unwitting betrayal of his spouse is merely the fruit of Hagen's insidious design to capture the ring. When Siegfried rode away from Brünnhilde, he traveled to the court of Gunther which, but for appearances, is truly Hagen's court; for the evil man entwines the fates of Gunther and his sister Gutrune like puppet strings about his fingers. Hagen has Gutrune give Siegfried a potion that causes him to forget Brünnhilde, and in fact all of his past life, as though it were blown to the winds. Suddenly, the boy yearns for Gutrune; she, too, is enamored of Siegfried. To Gunther, on the other hand, Hagen deceptively promises both Brünnhilde and, eventually, the ring. Having manipulated events to this point, Hagen suggests a double wedding, preceded by a firm oath of eternal brotherhood and loyalty between Siegfried and Gunther. Yet Siegfried alone possesses the "Tarnhelm," lending its wearer any shape desired, and he also is the only one who knows how to climb through the flames protecting his wife's abode. Thus, he himself must take on Gunther's form.

Siegfried performs his treacherous chore well, while the duped Gunther awaits him at the bottom of the mountain. Siegfried rips the ring from Brünnhilde's finger in much the way in which Wotan once tore it off Alberich's hand. Hagen now takes revenge for his father through his puppet. After seizing his once-beloved for Gunther, Siegfried precedes him to the wedding ceremony that Hagen is setting up in Act Two. Finally, Gunther leads in the bewildered "bride."

Brünnhilde's immense shock upon glimpsing her ring on Siegfried's hand turns into violent fury with the first realization of how hideously she has been deceived. Naturally, she blames Siegfried, who now behaves toward her as though she were a stranger, while still believing that it was the real Gunther who stole her ring. Yet Hagen, keen-eyed, controls the whole game as never before. Hagen tells Brünnhilde that if the events she watches here have actually occurred, then Siegfried is the culprit who won the gold by theft and mendacity; and that the faithless fellow shall pay for it. Siegfried, however, still claims that he knows nothing about all this. But his wife insists that she is right. Brünnhilde's love is changing to hate with a vengeance. Wagner could scarcely conceive a more graphic symbolization of the loss of personality and freedom through erotic love.

When the lighthearted and ignorant Siegfried disappears with Gutrune, Brünnhilde is alone with Hagen and Gunther. Very soon Hagen offers his services in slaying the hero, and Brünnhilde herself tells him where his spear can pierce him best. Siegfried can be stabbed only in the back; that is the single weak spot on his otherwise invulnerable body. "There," Hagen states, "my spear will strike!" Gunther's brain has turned into a twisting maze of uncertainty and despair. Now he calls on his half-brother Hagen to somehow help him out of his emotional squalor. Hagen mutters grimly that only Siegfried's death can help him. Beginning to suffocate at last beneath Hagen's menace, yet warmly reflecting his oath of brotherhood with Siegfried, Gunther bursts out: "Did he betray *me?*"

"Siegfried did betray you," Brünnhilde emphatically answers, "but all of you betrayed *me!* If I had justice, all the blood of this world would not wipe out your guilt! But the *one's* death will do me for all: let Siegfried fall—as an atonement for you and himself." Lifting Brünnhilde beyond the passion of her supreme hate, Wagner, for a moment, causes her to reveal Siegfried's fate as another repetition of the venerable archetype: the guilt-laden goat sent adrift in the wilderness on the Day of Atonement.

Heaped with the sins contrived by Hagen, Siegfried is slated to be cut down by the grim man's spear during a hunt on the next day. It is a ruse to appease Gunther's sickened conscience before Gutrune. "Let anguish and terror strike her!" Brünnhilde cries in awful loathing for herself and the world. On top of everything else, Hagen whispers to Gunther how the hero's death will be good for them all. Besides, the dark man insinuates, there is the promise of the ring's power, *if* Gunther can trick Siegfried out of it. As Act Two comes to an end and the plotters affirm faith in their atrocious deed, Wagner's orchestra feeds the swamp of deceit and vengeance on stage. "Love," has been turned completely upside down.

The events following prove the horror of that fact. Wandering away on the hunt, Siegfried meets the Rhine maidens, who flirt with him solely in the attempt to make him throw his ring to them. When he flauntingly refuses, they warn him that he will perish. In the presence of Gunther and the huntsmen, Hagen causes him to recall all the glories of Brünnhilde's awakening and his love for her. Hagen thus exposes Siegfried as a perjurer under his oath of brotherhood to Gunther. In this way, Hagen provides the legality of the hero's slaughter. When Siegfried turns his back, Hagen drives the weapon unerringly between his shoulder blades; just where Brünnhilde told him he could. The avenging angel screams: "I pay back perjury!" and stalks away.

Siegfried is dead. According to Wagner's stage directions, Gunther and his men mournfully lift the corpse upon a shield and carry it slowly off. In the revealing Bayreuth production of 1965, however, Wieland Wagner's version of this important episode may actually have been more to the point, highlighting the deeper significance of the scene. As the glow of full horns splendidly depicts the brighter moments in the hero's life, the body lies alone, an ignoble shell ungracefully sprawled on mid-stage. Not even in death does the body seem shielded from its murderer and the sordid happenings which he brings about in the next scene.

Hagen carries in Siegfried's corpse; and with no more feeling than if he were talking of a slain beast, he announces to the anxious Gutrune that he brings "the prey of a wild boar"; it is Gutrune's dead "husband." Endeavoring to comfort his sister, Gunther answers her terror-ridden grief by pointing to the cynical Hagen: "He is the loathsome boar who ripped the flesh of this noble youth!" "Are you mad at me for *that?*" exclaims Hagen insinuatingly. "May dread and misfortune seize you forever!" shouts Gunther, who at last is fully awake to his own share in the atrocity; but not for long. His insight scarcely blinds him to the brilliance of the gold that still gleams on the lifeless hand. With terrifying defiance, Hagen admits that he struck down the hero; and now he demands the time-honored right to the dead man's booty. Then he tries to grab the ring. But Gunther, hungering after the powerful metal himself, fights with his half-brother and is also slain. Finally unchallenged, Hagen reaches out for the prize, but the hand of the corpse rises in fearful warning.

Into this morass of sordidness and terror Brünnhilde enters monumentally. Her mind has become virtually cleansed of all notions about love's adequacy, just as it has been finally released from every illusion. With wisdom and identity at last regained, she is now impelled by the compassionate insight of old.

The Rhine maidens have indeed made known to her each detail
of Hagen's treachery and Siegfried's unwitting complicity. Moreover, "sorrowing love" has opened her eyes and compelled her to
view "the world's ending," precisely as Wagner has her announce
in the second variant conclusion to the drama, which he never set
to music. In the fullness of time, Brünnhilde may be said to have
learned to regard the world and its illusions much in the way that
Schopenhauer perceived them at the end of his *World as Will and
Idea*, when he states that the ultimate level of man's vision shall
be: "no will; no idea; no world" (*Kein Wille; keine Vorstellung;
keine Welt*).

Brünnhilde orders a funeral pyre to be raised up for the hero
Siegfried on the bank of the Rhine. She, too, yearns to be con-
sumed with him in the final flames. For the last time she addresses
the powers of the fading order: "Turn down your gaze upon my
blossoming sorrow," Brünnhilde commands, "behold your everlasting offense!"

> Lenkt euren Blick
> auf mein blühendes Leid:
> erschaut eure ewige Schuld!

It is the dooming judgment of Wotan's daughter and Siegfried's
grieving wife; yet with a profound compassion Brünnhilde tells
the god of the passing world to find eternal rest: "*Ruhe! Ruhe, du
Gott!—*"

Removing the ring from Siegfried's hand, Brünnhilde lets it be
known that the gold shall be returned to the Rhine maidens forever. Once again in their keeping and restored to the water's natural and indifferent element, the evil of the metal will be washed
away for all time.

The mistress of destiny now orders the consummation of *Götterdämmerung:* the physical eradication of a moribund universe
and of all its rulers shall be completed through fire. In truth, the
world shall return to that state of prime nothingness which pre-
vailed in an age before the World Ash. The Ash Tree itself was
destroyed in the far past, and Wotan's mighty spear, long ago torn
from the tree's ancient side, lies shattered.

The conflagration of the universe shall now come to pass exactly as the Norns once foresaw in the Prologue. Furnishing the

key to Wagner's myth from start to finish, the Prologue states: "Wotan digs deep the smashed spear's jagged splinters into the breast of the fire god. Searing flame seizes the torch; this the god casts into the Ash Tree's towering pyre of logs."

> Des zerschlagnen Speeres
> stechende Splitter
> taucht' einst Wotan
> dem Brünstigen tief in die Brust.
> Zehrender Brand
> zündet da auf;
> den wirft der Gott
> in der Weltesche
> zu Hauf geschichtete Scheite.

The end of Walhalla and of the rule of the everlasting gods was also foreseen: "Once the wood burns, blazing up fiercely and bright; once the furnace singes and swallows the glistening hall: the end of eternal gods eternally dawns."

> Brennt das Holz
> heilig brünstig und hell,
> sengt die Glut
> sehrend den glänzenden Saal:
> der ewigen Götter Ende
> dämmert ewig da auf.

In the beginning and the end was the World Ash Tree. Wagner's myth is rounded out; and his *Ring*, in a metaphorical sense, is closed. Nothing is redeemed. The audience is left staring into a void that might be filled only by Schopenhauer's bracing pessimism concerning man's lasting predicament: "Ahead of us lies, to be sure, nothing at all" (*Vor uns steht allerdings nur das Nichts*). There remains solely the assurance of man's hopeless and limitless frustration. It is the endless frustration of man who attempts to gather seeds of sense from indifferent and hostile nature, and from himself. Frustration and nothingness. Why, then, did Wagner even bother to conceive the *Ring* at all? Obviously, only by working through the entire problem could he begin even to grasp it; or, better, endure to grasp it.

Aside from carving a chronological mythology out of what is

our timeless human condition, Wagner managed to make from
the *Ring's* music a kind of myth as well. For just as he contrived to
have us believe that the sustained, single note—an acoustic idea
of creation—with which *Das Rheingold* opens as from the abyss
of time, has been there always; so now, at the very last, when only
water and fire fill up the stage, he causes us to feel, perhaps only
for a moment, that our human state and time itself have simply
ceased to be. It is this musical image which explains, in part, the
quasi-religious aura that people frequently associate with performances of *Die Götterdämmerung* or its concluding scene.

It is odd that audiences should feel elated by the annihilation of
things. Yet that triumph is Wagner's; it is the triumph of perceiving that any notion about the final adequacy of nature or society,
of erotic love or freedom, can only be a deception. At the end, the
Ring even suggests that you cannot be free *and* human. The destinies of Wotan and Brünnhilde, of Siegmund and Siegfried, appear
to bear out that contention.

But if man is unable to create freedom or an adequate society,
if erotic love is exposed as a destructive and ephemeral illusion,
and if man and nature remain utterly unredeemable, then empathy alone survives. From this point on, it continues to be seen as
the single cohesive element within the social bond, in the same
way in which it is viewed as the sole ground for value within a
reality that is intrinsically without value, order, and significance.

Richard Wagner's reassessment of society, freedom, and love,
however, led him a considerable distance beyond Tristan's and
Brünnhilde's negation. The last two works he conceived, *Die
Meistersinger von Nürnberg* (1862–67) and *Parsifal* (1877–82),
bear incontestable witness to the course along which his agonizing
reappraisal of value was guiding him.

CHAPTER 5

Baptism and Shoes

IN *The Concise Oxford Dictionary of Opera,* we find the following informative tidbit concerning Wagner's next-to-last creation: "Wagner here celebrates the virtues of a bourgeois morality to which his whole life ran counter. . . . *Meistersinger* is an opera that persuades the listener of the goodness not of gods or heroes or ideals, but simple men." [1] Except in the most literal and superficial sense, none of this is true. But it is one more example of the type of criticism and comment that for long has marred the comprehension of Wagner the artist. In the end, it remains as glib as it is shallow and uninformative.

In his *Die Meistersinger von Nürnberg* (The Mastersingers of Nuremberg), Wagner could not be less concerned with depicting a "bourgeois" or "normal" world any more than he tries to persuade us of the "goodness" of simple mortals, or of anyone else. Moreover, Wagner proves to be essentially disinterested in either the Mastersingers or in Nuremberg. To believe otherwise is to confuse the eggshell with the yolk.

Die Meistersinger is really all about art, illusion, and erotic love; and on another rather important level it is even about Tristan and Isolde. The astonishingly elaborate mantle Wagner deftly weaves from these ideas, interlacing their multiple strands through the metaphors of baptism and shoemaking, remains one of the wonders of art. In its scope and profundity, the myth of Nürnberg and its shoemaker is equal to the World Ash Tree mythology of the *Ring*. The ultimate configuration of *Die Meistersinger* is in fact so incredibly perfected that the colorful panorama of sixteenth-century Nuremberg and its guilds—which it ostensibly is—ends by becoming one of the most complicated and misunderstood works of art ever seen.

The significant theme of baptism is stressed from the very outset. On the day before the Feast of St. John (*Johannistag*) within

Nuremberg's famous church of St. Catherine, a chorale in honor
of John the Baptist is sung by the congregation. The specifically
Wagnerian import of this hymn comes to light in the words addressed to St. John: "Noble baptizer! Christ's forerunner!" (*Edler
Täufer! Christs Vorläufer!*). For Wagner, St. John is no other than
Johannes ("Hans") Sachs of Nuremberg and the central personage of Wagner's myth, who lived from 1494 to 1576 and was a
shoemaker, in addition to being one of the most prolific writers in
Germany during the sixteenth century.

While the congregation sings, young Walter von Stolzing stands
impatiently at the church entrance, trying to catch the attention of
Eva who, as it develops, is to become his bride the following day.
He makes her closer acquaintance as the parishioners leave. She
exits soon afterwards with Magdalene, her friend and escort;
whereupon Walter meets David, the youthful apprentice of Hans
Sachs. David informs Walter about all the varied and complex
rules of the Mastersingers' Guild. But Walter shows himself to be
absolutely ignorant even of the least part thereof. He replies nega-
tively to each of David's queries and confesses his total ignorance
of every important technical question and term relating to the
venerable art. In this way, Wagner from the very start graphically
characterizes the young knight as a new stage in the evolution of
the guileless simpleton. Walter's prototype was Siegfried, and its
more successful continuation will be Parsifal.

We frankly expect Wagner to load all his dice in favor of Walter
and his mentor Hans Sachs from the beginning. Walter is indeed
characterized as the ingenuous, *natural* artist who, despite his ignorance of the sophisticated Masters' art and its numerous rules—
or precisely because of his ignorance—is best fitted to evolve from
a naïvely exuberant but undisciplined genius into a mature and
disciplined Mastersinger and a highly original artist in his own
right, an artist who finally knows every last trick of the trade.
Wagner himself learned to do as much. That in terms of theatrical
chronology Walter von Stolzing learns to do all of this in less than
twenty-four hours only makes Wagner's non-chronological ab-
straction—his myth—all the more emphatic and significant. Once
again, to continue the metaphor, Wagner's yolk has very little
to do with the theatrical, and chronological, egg shell he is using.
Yet the historical details of the surface, especially those involving
the rules and the forms of Master Singing (*Meistergesang*) are so

thoroughly authentic that they may be profitably used by students of that subject.[2]

After David has explained to Walter many of the technical and artistic terms of the guild, the Masters themselves enter the church. They have come to hold their customary weekly meeting; but this time Walter von Stolzing is present. He tells them that he has left his ancestral estate in Franconia and has come to Nuremberg "only out of love for art." He also informs the Masters that he, too, desires to become a Master and enter their guild.

Veit Pogner tells his assembled colleagues about the song contest to be held on the following day, the Feast of St. John, before the entire populace. To the Masters' surprise, Pogner announces that he, a wealthy citizen, will give the hand of his only daughter Eva in marriage, together with a considerable dowry, to the winner. Pogner's stipulation, however, is that only the one whom the Masters have selected shall marry Eva.

Hans Sachs objects to these terms from the start. He feels that Pogner's plan compromises the nature of genuine art by the placing of the final decision in the hands of the Masters alone. If Pogner really desires to demonstrate how highly art is esteemed, then the folk themselves, along with Eva and the Masters, must be made the judges. Eva's own choice of winner and husband, Sachs feels, will naturally accord with the opinion of the whole people. The Masters show uneasiness about this unorthodox notion. They believe that it would jeopardize their dignity and artistic tradition and would weaken the authority of their ancient, sacrosanct rules involving the singer's complex craft. For all these rules have long been carefully guarded and zealously upheld in the *Tabulatur,* which is that hallowed catalogue of complicated forms and regulations governing all Master-Songs.

Hans Sachs, however, is of a different opinion. He tells his colleagues that for many years he himself has striven to preserve their sacred *Tabulatur.* Yet now his view has changed: at least once a year each regulation ought to be closely re-examined. For all these rules have to be tested over and over again, Sachs insists, against both habit and time, so that one may decide whether they have lost some of their marrow and force; and whether they still appear to be natural and artistically wholesome. This significant task can be undertaken solely by him "who *knows nothing* about the *Tabulatur.*" This appears to be the condition for an art that will please the whole folk: the community is the ultimate judge of art, and the Masters must descend from their lofty cloud to consult *them.*

In effect, what Hans Sachs is proposing is a reformation, but scarcely a wholesale revolt. Real change and, with it, new values, must be introduced from the outside, at least by someone from outside the community that, Sachs implies, has become barren of value in its traditions. In much the same manner, in fact, Catholic Nuremberg was renovated from the outside by the Reformation of Martin Luther.

It is obvious that the Hans Sachs of Wagner's myth is supposed to function in the same way in which the Hans Sachs of history once did when he penned his famous praise of Luther and his incipient Reformation in the allegorical verses of "The Wittenberg Nightingale" (*Die Wittembergisch Nachtigall*). Composed in 1523, this poem extols the bird heralding the new dawn, representing Martin Luther himself. In the final scene of Act Three, Wagner makes the meaning of his own allegory, whose basis is the allusion to Luther by the historical Hans Sachs, more than apparent, as soon as the people pay vocal homage to *Wagner's* "Baptist" Hans Sachs, who then baptizes the renovator of art, Walter von Stolzing. This occurs when they sing the opening lines of the authentic Nightingale poem once composed by the historical Sachs.

All of this turns, therefore, into a kind of double allegory: Wagner's own allegory dealing with the reformation of art, appears in a double guise: that of the original allegory involving Hans Sachs and Martin Luther's Reformation, and the direct symbolization of Sachs and Walter, respectively, as John the Baptist and Christ. The new "Nightingale" is, of course, none other than Walter von Stolzing who, at the end, delivers the Master Song whose creation the shoemaker has carefully guided and then "baptized."

Before the Masters assembled in St. Catherine's Church, Hans Sachs elaborates the metaphor of baptism that we saw introduced by the parishioners when the curtain opened. Now the wise shoemaker insists that each year, on the Feast of St. John, the august Masters should not merely condescend to have the folk attend the annual Singers' contest; rather, they themselves should turn to the folk in order to judge *whether art pleases them.* "It is the opinion of Hans Sachs," he proclaims, "that the folk and its art ought to blossom and develop hand in hand."

Dass Volk und Kunst gleich blüh' und wachs',
bestellt ihr so, mein' ich, Hans Sachs.

At this important juncture, the Feast of St. John vividly prefigures the Wagnerian notion of the consecration of novel value through art. In Wagner's myth, John the Baptist's consecration of Christ, Hans Sachs's consecration of Luther's Reformation in the Nightingale poem, and finally the shoemaker's consecration of Walter's Prize Song are seen to function analogously. What in sixteenth-century Nuremberg actually signified an impending cultural and religious crisis, becomes—in Wagnerian perspective—a cultural problem that has to be solved.

Where does the task of religion intersect with that of art? Or does it do so at all? The only relevant point is that in *Die Meistersinger*, as in *Tannhäuser, Lohengrin,* and the *Ring,* Wagner is merely exploiting what remains for him yet another outworn mythology (in this instance: dead historical facts) as a supreme myth of his own. The idea of baptism, therefore, is to be taken no more seriously in its own right than, say, the World Ash Tree.

As a matter of fact, by 1880, in the essay *Art and Religion* Wagner finally divulged the direction in which his religious views had moved all along. "One could say," he begins, "that when religion becomes artificial, it remains for art to salvage its true essence by perceiving its mythical symbols—which religion would have us believe as the literal truth—only according to their figurative value, in order to make us see their profound, hidden truth through idealized representation."[3] By "idealized representation" Wagner means, of course, theatrical art, especially his own. Wagner is also implying that his art may exploit religion, history, and mythology, or any combination of these, as part of a personal esthetic strategy. In adopting this point of view, he is scarcely different from most of the advanced artists of his century.

Before the assembly of Masters, Walter von Stolzing presents a laudable but undisciplined account of his "art" in the song "On the Quiet Hearth." Walter's effort demonstrates every conceivable transgression against the sacred regulations of the *Tabulatur,* as these are officially judged by the conscientious "Marker of errors," Sixtus Beckmesser. Because of his mistakes, Walter is promptly disqualified. Everyone assents except Hans Sachs, who remains the only one to find words of praise for the originality and integrity of the song; for as Sachs tells the dissenting Masters, the song "was new, but it was not confused." He then goes on to compare Walter with himself: if Sachs can make verses *and* shoes, then the naïve young artist can be both a knight and a poet. But at this stage nobody is listening to Hans Sachs. What the shoemaker is actually saying at the end of Act One is that Walter von Stolzing could be, in fact, a new Hans Sachs.

Throughout the second act, Wagner develops his shoe metaphor in much greater detail. Ultimately, however, this metaphor is seen to be quite inseparable from that of baptism, since both represent the notion of the revitalization of time-worn forms and discarded values; at least of values discarded by Hans Sachs. Yet between baptism and shoemaking there is a difference; whereas the former is seen as a metaphor for renovation through art, the metaphor of shoemaking can be viewed as being rather more sustained. It stands for the idea of the artist directing all the roles and illusions of the people toward more noble ends, in the same spirit that Richard Wagner himself hoped his own works might one day do. That is the essential meaning of Hans Sachs's mission as a "shoemaker and a poet, too," precisely as he himself informs us. The terms of the shoemaker's trade never occur in *Die Meistersinger* without metaphorical significance; this is also the case with the theme of baptism.

The first manipulation of illusion toward "nobler ends" takes place in the second act. Sachs has discovered that Eva loves the young man she had met after church that afternoon; but he tells her that nothing prevents the elderly and ridiculous Beckmesser from winning her in the contest the next day. But he hopes to make the proper shoes for Beckmesser on St. John's eve, just as he claims that Eva's shoes will certainly be fit for a lovely bride to wear.

As a Nuremberg shoemaker, however, Hans Sachs soon realizes that he has an immediate and more difficult task to fulfill. Seated at his cobbler's bench, he quickly discovers that the young lovers are about to take matters into their own hands. With the threat of Beckmesser as a successful wooer before her, Eva, in Walter's arms but within earshot of the listening Sachs, impetuously decides to elope with her youthful knight. But Hans Sachs is ahead of them both. Taking up his shoemaker's hammer and a song, he composes a tale about Eve's fall from Paradise, in order to guide the illusions of the real Eva within hearing range. Sachs relates that when Eve was thrust out of Paradise by the Lord, the hard gravel hurt her bare feet. That made the dear Lord sorry, for he liked her little feet. So He called on an angel, commanding: "Go ahead and make the poor sinner some shoes. And since Adam, as I see, is bumping his barefooted toes against rocks, measure boots for him, too, so that from here on he can travel properly!"

It is obvious that Sachs is describing himself in the role of the angel; he is saying that he must sole both Walter and Eva so that they can cope with reality and its responsibilities with maturity, exactly as the Lord's angel had done for Adam and Eve in the myth. In the second stanza of his song, Sachs claims that it lies heavily on Eve's conscience that angels now have to make shoes for people. If she had stayed in Paradise, there would be no hard gravel to worry about. That is, Sachs continues, "because of your misdeed" in leaving the paternal home to elope with Walter, "I manipulate the awl and thread" to set matters aright. And he concludes that "because of Adam's human weakness I sole shoes and smooth over bad luck by using cobbler's pitch." No English phrase is able to convey the pithiness and aptness of Wagner's play on words in the last phrase: "smooth over bad luck by using cobbler's pitch." The German is simply *streiche Pech*, which means both. The last section of this stanza, as summarized above, is:

> Ob deiner jungen Missetat
> hantier' ich jetzt mit Ahl' und Draht,
> und ob Herrn Adams übler Schwäch'
> versohl' ich Schuh' und streiche Pech.

Wagner repeatedly employs double meaning, as we might expect, for the shoemaker's *wax* and *pitch* throughout this act.

In the third stanza, Sachs states that the world does not recognize the importance either of the shoemaker or the poet. That is simply because the artist, unlike most individuals and communities, clearly perceives the world's illusions; and only by applying the artist's craft to his poetic vision may he control illusion for the people's benefit, much in the way Wagner thought he himself was doing. That is what Sachs means when he says that he is "a shoe-

maker and a poet, too." By controlling all of the mechanical
means of his art, he can form a bridge between what his artistic
vision perceives as illusion and what the folk willingly accept on
tradition and faith. In Act Three, Sachs begins to teach Walter to
do precisely this. Walter, in other words, learns from Sachs how
he may control "Paradise" (his love for Eva) in order that it may
be perceived as illusion in terms of art, what Wagner later calls
Parnassus.

At the beginning of the last act, Wagner explicitly associates
Hans Sachs with John the Baptist, finally elucidating what had
only been intimated in the chorale that opens Act One. David
enters Sachs's workshop and exclaims that today they are celebrat-
ing the Feast Day of St. John. He then sings a verse that Hans
Sachs undoubtedly himself composed: "On the river Jordan, St.
John stood to baptize all the world's people. A foreign woman
came there too, journeying all the way from Nuremberg. She bore
her little son to the shore's edge and received the child's baptism
and his name. But when they turned homeward and found themselves in Nuremberg once more, they discovered that whoever on
the river Jordan was called 'John' on Nuremberg's river Pegnitz
was named 'Hans' as well." David punctuates his song by exclaiming that today is his master's name day. He hands him the
flowers he is holding and asks Sachs if he would like to try some
of the sausage he is carrying.

Once again we have a graphic display of the dramatist's exploitation of history and legend for the aims of his own original myth,
which includes his total disregard for the integrity of his sources.
Indeed, Hans Sachs will soon assume the role of baptist when he
consecrates the final version of Walter's song, thus paralleling the
historical St. John's baptism of Christ, as well as the re-consecra-
tion of value performed by Luther in the day of the historical
Hans Sachs. In the last act, when Nuremberg's populace takes up
the poem of the real Sachs in praise of Luther in order to honor
Wagner's hero, this notion of parallel function becomes strongly
emphasized.

After David's departure, Hans Sachs begins his important monologue on *Wahn*, which, we recall, signifies the idea of illusion,
deception, or fancy. In the present context, however, the shoemaker is referring mainly to illusion, and to the major role it plays
in the life and imagination of mankind. Illusion, Hans Sachs be-

gins, is all about us: "*Wahn, Wahn! Überall Wahn!*" Nothing, he adds, happens without it. If it is arrested in its course, it only grows in strength; *Wahn* must in fact be brought under control and mastered: "A cobbler in his shop pulls on the threads of *Wahn.*" ("*Ein Schuster in seinem Laden/zieht an des Wahnes Faden.*") "Let us see," Sachs continues, "how Hans Sachs goes about controlling illusion in order to bring about more noble works. If he does not allow us rest, even here in Nuremberg let it be because of such deeds which seldom are successful when performed by ordinary means, and never succeed without the help of some *Wahn.*"

> Jetzt schaun wir, wie Hans Sachs es macht,
> dass er den Wahn fein lenken mag,
> ein edler' Werk zu tun;
> denn lässt er uns nicht ruhn,
> selbst hier in Nürenberg,
> so sei's um solche Werk',
> die selten vor gemeinen Dingen,
> und nie ohn' ein'gen Wahn gelingen.

Worth considering is the fact that even though Hans Sachs has penetrated illusion and is thus able to stand above it and direct it, he never seeks to use his wisdom as a basis for moral authority. He does not even suggest that he possesses such authority, but merely faces himself with complete objectivity by frequently regarding himself in the third person as "Hans Sachs." The shoemaker only claims that "Hans Sachs" is in a position to direct illusion and deception toward more noble ends. What Wagner and Sachs are actually talking about is that illusion is ennobled, best of all, through art.

Hans Sachs knows that illusion and petty self-deceptions set the tone of most experiences and can be regarded as the principal mode of man's existence. Behind man's reliance on deception and illusion lurks the definite need of some authority, natural or divine. But Sachs—even though he might easily do so—refuses to recognize his own authority; and that is exactly the point. On the other hand, the shoemaker truly believes in the sacredness of art because he knows that the artist alone—by means of his imagination and the exercise of it through artistic control—releases value by freeing man from the necessity for illusion. Art means freedom, and thus value, simply because it demands no illusory authority whatever. In the artist's mind, accordingly, imagination redeems the world because the perceptive mind of the artist is able to view experiential reality as symbolic. Hans Sachs is really saying, therefore, that the artist is able directly to engage with reality only because he alone perceives, and can employ, *artistic* illusions that are actually the symbols of experience. From this notion emerges the ultimate significance of "shoes," as well as the true meaning of Sachs's remark that he is "a shoemaker and a poet, too."

By 1864, when Wagner was already far along with his *Meistersinger,* he inferred much of this in the essay *The State and Religion.* Art, Wagner writes, is a noble deception, an illusion that "must be totally forthright; from the very outset it must admit that it is a deception." [4] The task of art, then, is benevolently to resolve reality into an illusion, so that art may ultimately be seen for what it really is: pure symbol. The distress and the earnestness of reality, together with its joys, will then appear to us, in turn, admittedly as illusion. "The meaninglessness of the world," Wagner concludes, "will then be made apparent, harmless, and confessed as though with smiles: for the very fact that we have desired to be deceived led us on to perceive the world's reality without deceptions of any kind." [5]

With such important insights, Wagner stood in the very forefront of cultural developments in mid-nineteenth-century Europe. In his *Beyond the Tragic Vision,* Morse Peckham accentuates this fact by saying: "In precisely those years when Wagner was working on *Die Meistersinger,* Robert Browning, the English poet, was saying the same thing in *The Ring and the Book.* Art is 'true' because it is a lie and doesn't pretend to be anything else. Art cannot redeem the world, but it can give the man who looks at the world the experience of value. By manipulating illusions and releasing the power of art, Hans Sachs establishes a relation among the artist, the people, and the holders of social power. The power of art is now clear." [6]

In the scene that immediately follows the shoemaker's monologue on *Wahn,* Walter himself is informed by Hans Sachs that art is the noblest of illusions. The youthful poet tells Sachs that he has just had "a wondrously beautiful dream," from which he now has awakened refreshed. The older man encourages Walter to relate all of it. Nonetheless, Walter replies that he hardly dares to think about it; for he fears that the dream will evade him and fade from memory. Hans Sachs, however, admonishes him by saying that it is precisely the poet's task to note and interpret his dreaming: "Believe me, man's truest *Wahn* is revealed to him in dreams: all creativity and poetizing is nothing more than the articulation and interpretation of the meaningful dream" (*Wahrtraum-Deuterei*). If Walter can relate his "Morning Dream," Sachs says, he will be able to instruct him in the rules that will guide the ultimate artistic expression of the dream. Walter asks him whether this would not be poetry rather than dreaming? But Sachs asserts that they are friends who assist each other willingly. It is, of course, Wagner himself who is speaking.

In this conversation between the shoemaker and his pupil, Wagner, in fact, lays bare what ostensibly are his own views on artistic creation and its whole reason for being. Wagner does this by showing how Hans Sachs prunes the young man's ardent feelings of first love by directing them along a path that will produce a work of art—the Morning Song—through disciplined creativity. The notion emerges that the significant difference between a true artist and the mere entertainer, or "inspired" singer, is a qualitative one. That becomes clear when Sachs remarks that although many people actually succeed in producing lovely songs when their hearts glow with a first love, such people merely succeed because the springtime itself sings those songs *for* them. Yet if one hopes to develop into a genuine artist, one must be able to compose beautiful songs about love at any time, whether it may be spring or summer, winter or fall, and in spite of the joys and sorrows of everyday. The shoemaker emphasizes that this capability marks the true artist, because he knows how to use the rules and technique of his art so well that even if love and its springtime have long run their course for him, he is still able to freshen up the image of love and spring as often and as effectively as he likes.

Hans Sachs gives young Walter some insight into the processes of art and, in doing this, begins to tame a little of Walter's exuberance. "How am I to start," he now significantly asks, "according to the rules?" "You make them up yourself, and then follow them. Just recall your lovely Morning Dream, and let Hans Sachs take care of all the rest," Sachs states, referring to himself as shoemaker and poet once more in the third person.

Walter commences to relate his dream in song, while Hans Sachs sits with paper and ink to write it down; in this way he bends Walter's inspiration to the rules of art while yet allowing him to give these rules a fresh meaning all his own. The rules of the *Tabulatur* require that Walter deliver a song consisting of three parts: two *Stollen* and one *Abgesang*. This means roughly that the final poem shall be made up of two primary stanzas, followed by a concluding stanza in a differing form.

The first two *Stollen* describe the golden fruit on the tree of life, which is Eva. Sachs immediately begins to manipulate the form as well as the content of the youngster's inspiration. He maintains, first of all, that Walter has achieved such a perfect fusion of dream and poetic vision that Sachs can no longer distinguish one basic element from the other. In the melody, however, the young man is still a bit too free. This is hardly an error, Sachs proclaims, and yet a melody that is not simple to memorize—and here Wagner is digging at some critics' views of his own melodies—"irritates our old men." The shoemaker therefore requests Walter to compose a second stanza.

The first stanza concluded with a description of Eva's hand beckoning toward what the young lover yearned for: the valuable and lovely fruit on the tree of life (*Lebensbaum*). In contrast to this, however, the poet-lover, in the second stanza, depicts his beloved Eva exactly in the way in which Tristan and Isolde painted one another's image. That is to say, Walter now depicts Eva erotically in terms of the departing day and the enshrouding night. This is not inappropriate, for Walter does in fact view Eva in a "night-sighted" way, just as in the second act of *Tristan* the hero says that he beholds Isolde in a "night-sighted" vision. In this second stanza Walter also employs a phrase from the love scene of *Tristan und Isolde,* in order to portray Eva's eyes as, "glowing like two bright stars from a distance [which] appear so near, yet are so far."

A comparison of two passages reveals this significant parallel. Tristan refers to Isolde's presence in Act Two with these words: "So far and yet so near! So near and yet so far!" (*Wie weit so nah!/ So nah wie weit!*) The German for Walter's phrase in the second stanza is as follows (italics mine):

Wie weit so nah
beschienen da
zwei lichte Sterne
aus der Ferne

The vocabulary alone of this second version provides so many similarities with the lovers' vocabulary in *Tristan und Isolde* that we are constrained to seek Wagner's deliberate intent in the matter. Moreover, Wagner's idea would be correct: Walter in fact is still very much in the Tristanesque stages of his attachment. Hans Sachs-Wagner knows this and attempts to divert the tide not in a different direction, but rather over new beds. One could argue that the evolution of Walter's Prize Song is autobiographical, for it clearly reflects Wagner's own inward evolution from *Tristan* to *Die Meistersinger*, from the notion of erotic love as a supreme value to the idea that love, like most other illusions, can be redeemed by art.

Yet by the end of the second stanza Walter's emotional surge begins to be controlled by art. This is evident when the final line of the first *Abgesang* about the "lovely fruit on the tree of life" is altered significantly to: "rather than fruit—a sea of stars on the laurel tree [*Lorbeerbaum*]." This new image is not only more abstract and less earthy, it is far more self-consciously esthetic as well. Eva's eyes now become a host of stars, while the tree of life develops into a symbol of artistic success, the emblem of victory itself: the laurel tree. All of this now specifically supplants the earthly "fruit." The concluding lines of the two versions ought to be compared for this crucial alteration.

FIRST VERSION

. . . mit Augen winkend,
die Hand wies blinkend,
was ich verlangend begehrt,
die Frucht so hold und wert
vom Lebensbaum.

SECOND VERSION

. . . zu Tanz und Reigen
in Laub und Zweigen
der goldnen sammeln sich mehr,
statt Frucht ein Sternenheer
im Lorbeerbaum.

The important change shows the youthful poet, under the omnis-
cient guidance of Hans Sachs, slowly advancing spiritually from a
realm of endless night and the supremacy of unconscious feeling
into the objective dimension of art, with its careful perception and
control of feelings and illusions.

Nonetheless, Walter von Stolzing is not yet quite prepared for
evidence of complete maturity. To Sachs's suggestion to compose
a third bar that would entirely clarify the artistic interpretation of
the dream, Walter replies only with impatience. How would he
discover such a thing? He ends by exclaiming that he has had
enough of words.

At Sachs's suggestion Walter accompanied by the shoemaker
retires to another room, in order to change into full attire for the
coming contest. Sixtus Beckmesser then enters the shop. Seeing no
one present, the "Marker of errors" craftily spies Walter's half-
completed song lying on the desk where Sachs had left it. Believing it to be the song with which Sachs plans to woo Eva, the
rascal puts it in his pocket. Shortly afterwards, Hans Sachs, ar-
rayed in festive garments, re-enters the room. At first he thinks
that Beckmesser is visiting him again because of his shoes. "I imagine they fit you well enough," Sachs exclaims. "The devil they
do," Beckmesser insists. "My soles were never so thin; I feel the
smallest stone through them." But the shoemaker jestingly re-
proves Beckmesser's chiding when he insinuates that the condition
of his shoes only reflects his meager talent. At this point, Wagner's
shoe metaphor begins to disclose varied dramatic situations. This
metaphor clearly signifies the adequacy of the person concerned in
meeting the demands of reality.

In the end, Hans Sachs makes Beckmesser a gift of Walter's still
unfinished song. Sachs need not be afraid to do so; for the song
can best be sung by him on whom "the shoes" fit really well. The
shoemaker realizes that in full public the "Marker" is likely to
make utter hash of his new song. Nonetheless, Beckmesser is over-
joyed by the unexpected gift; and as he leaves he yells out his
hope "that Nuremberg will henceforth bloom and blossom in its
shoes!"

Eva now enters the shoemaker's shop. Having come there, she
exclaims, because of a "pinching shoe," the cobbler immediately
guesses what the trouble is. It is nothing more than the girl's fear

that her beloved Walter might fail in the coming contest, and that she might therefore become the victim of Beckmesser's successful wooing. But Hans Sachs knows better; that is why Eva's pinching shoe does not seem to bother him. The young lady, however, grows desperate at his callousness and blurts out: "Oh, Master Sachs! You know better than I where the shoe pinches me!"

Precisely at this moment—and with stunning dramatic effect—Eva utters a delighted cry when she beholds Walter entering the room, gorgeously attired for his coming victory. As Sachs removes the shoe for "repairs," Eva and her knight regard one another blissfully, while the girl's foot remains absentmindedly on the cobbler's stool. Now, the shoemaker is occupied in a different way. It annoys him, he says, that shoemaking alone seems to be his lot: day and night his work never lets up. Perhaps, he muses, looking Walter's way, a third stanza might now be ready?

While the cobbler diligently labors on the shoe, the young man bursts forth with the new stanza of his Master Song. The connection between the two is clear: Walter is beginning to learn to "fix shoes" in his own way. He is grasping the idea of how to do what Hans Sachs does. Walter, in other words, is learning to control and direct his personal feelings on the level of art.

Walter now sings that the laurel wreath lit up by the sunbeams from Eva's eyes grew pale but bloomed anew: "With this she crowns my head with artist's love and artist's fame, and into the poet's breast she pours the joy of Paradise." It is important to keep in mind the artist's image of erotic love, represented here by "Paradise," in order to appreciate its transformation in the ultimate version of Walter's Prize Song during the final moments of the drama. Sachs now tells Eva that she is hearing the song of a Master, and as he places the shoe on her foot he asks if it still "pinches." Hans Sachs has been conditioning her feet all along, and not merely in regard to the young man she loves. He has also prepared her for her own mature role in life. Eva's building up by Sachs, which began with his verses about Adam and Eve, is now completed, as the shoemaker places the fully mended shoe on her foot.

Eva realizes this. She tells her "friend Sachs" that she can never repay him for showing her such affection and empathy. What, indeed, would she have become without him. "Through you," she informs him, "I awoke. Through you alone I learned to think nobly, and with freedom and boldness; you allowed me to blossom!" For the moment emotionally swayed, and fearful still for Walter's success in the contest, Eva impetuously offers Hans Sachs her hand. But Sachs counters her pleasing proposal in the manner we might expect. He wants nothing of passion, for he is familiar enough with the tragic destiny of Tristan and Isolde. "Hans Sachs," he concludes, "is wise, and wants nothing of the luck of our dear friend Mark." Wagner even underscores this remark with the quotation of the main theme from *Tristan und Isolde;* thus quoting himself and, at the same time, strongly emphasizing his own evolution beyond the problem of that work. We may say that Hans Sachs, speaking about himself once again in third person, pellucidly mirrors Wagner's own hope of preserving detachment and peace from illusion, *i.e.,* of maintaining *Wahnfried.*[7] The quotation from *Tristan* gives one solid ground for believing that Walter's verbal reminiscence of that work earlier, in the second stanza of his song, was just as intentional on Wagner's part as the musical reference to it is now. The entire point is too deliberate to be missed: art, not death, redeems love; for art alone is able to sustain it.

By this time, Hans Sachs has provided proper shoes for both Eva and Walter. Now, having implanted in Eva a firm sense of identity and responsibility, and having produced within Walter a commanding perception of the way value emerges through art, and how love is sustained by it, Hans Sachs, maker and mender of shoes, prepares at last to assume explicitly the role of John the Baptist, in order to consecrate Walter and his renovating task.

What has been slowly evolved by shoes is now consummated through baptism. Wagner emphasizes that idea by completing the baptism metaphor—introduced, we recall, at the very opening of the curtain in Act One—when he has Sachs intone his consecration of Walter's newborn song to a familiar and chant-like cadence, actually employed from the sixteenth century until today in the high service of the Lutheran church. *Parsifal* can be said to begin right here. It is here that Wagner starts to use the illusions familiar to the actors on stage *as well as* those of the attending audience. The liturgical, chant-like theme Sachs uses in this baptism scene is—and is intended to be—as automatically conno-

tative to Wagner's audiences in 1868 and today as it was in mid-
sixteenth-century Nuremberg. It is an ingenious bit of sleight-of-
hand, a trick that Wagner exploits with incredible dexterity
throughout his next and final work.

Hans Sachs baptizes Walter's art by christening his new melody
"the theme interpreting the Morning Dream" (*die selige Morgen-
traumdeut-Weise*). It thus becomes also a symbol of reformation,
of a new day. Hans Sachs predicts that it shall receive the Masters' prize, as indeed in Wagner's myth it must.

With a change of scene, we are transported to a meadow outside the old walls of Nuremberg. There, on St. John's Day, the
annual contest takes place. First, the picturesque guilds of the town,
the shoemakers, the tailors, and the bakers, march in, with all
of their standards and their apprentices. Finally the Mastersingers
themselves appear. When Hans Sachs steps forward to inaugurate
the annual proceedings, the huge crowd addresses him with a
single, mighty voice: "Awake! The day approaches . . . the night
draws on toward the Occident, the day rises in the Orient. The
fiery red dawn moves on through the dismal clouds." The words
are taken from the opening of the poem about "The Wittenberg
Nightingale" written by the historical Hans Sachs. They extol "a
rapturous nightingale whose voice pierces mountain and valley."
The singing bird is Martin Luther, but it is also Hans Sachs.

Counting on the popularity of Sachs, Beckmesser hopes to
outdo any competitor with the aid of the song he tried to steal
from the cobbler's desk. Beckmesser even insinuates that if he
fails, Sachs will be to blame. After receiving the jeers and laughter
of the whole population for his garbled and idiotic rendition of
Walter's masterpiece, Beckmesser actually credits Sachs with its
authorship. The shoemaker momentarily appears to be in a tight
bind, until he insists that the song the people have just heard is
beautiful indeed. Walter von Stolzing, he announces, will prove
it.

The folk's "Nightingale" homage to Hans Sachs has celebrated
the triumph of the day over night. Now, the final version of the
Prize Song, in a context paralleling it, recounts the triumph of
Hans Sachs-Walter-Eva over Tristan's and Isolde's "night," and of
the artist's "laurel tree" over the "dream of love." That is to say,
the new "day" of art now redeems love because it is able to surpass
it by control and transfiguration.

The two *Stollen* and the *Abgesang* of Walter's Prize Song evolve as follows:

I. Morning: The artist is invited into the garden of Paradise where he beholds the "dream of love" (*Liebestraum*), which is Eve in Paradise:

> . . . ein Garten lud mich ein,
> dort unter einem Wunderbaum
> von Früchten reich behangen,
> zu schaun im sel'gen Liebestraum,
> was höchstem Lustverlangen
> Erfüllung kühn verhiess
> das schönste Weib,
> Eva im Paradies.

II. Evening–Night: A steep path leads the artist to the very source of art triumphant, which is represented by the *noble* wave. Here, the magic tree (*Wunderbaum*) in the first *Stollen* becomes the tree symbolizing artistic triumph, that is, the laurel tree (*Lorbeerbaum*). And the dream of Eros, the *Liebestraum*, now changes into a vision of the true poet: *Dichtertraum*. But what is most significant, the lovely figure that had been Eve in Paradise evolves into the Muse of Art, *die Muse des Parnass:*

> Abendlich dämmernd umschloss mich die Nacht;
> auf steilem Pfad
> war ich genaht
> wohl einer Quelle
> edler Welle,
> die lockend mir gelacht:
> dort unter einem Lorbeerbaum,
> von Sternen hell durchschienen,
> ich schaut' im wachen Dichtertraum,
> mit heilig holden Mienen
> mich netzend mit dem Nass,
> das hehrste Weib—
> die Muse des Parnass.

III. Dawn–New Day: The poet awakens from the artist's dream to behold Paradise transformed by renewed splendor. Art as the prime source of value becomes real. The "source" from which sprang "the noble wave" (*die Quelle edler Welle*), has shown him the path. "*Die wonnig wogende Welle*" of *Siegfried* and *Tristan* is now seen to be transfigured through art. Walter says that he is now consecrated to the Muse, who is earth's loveliest vision and whom he had wooed before. The "night," then, finally has been overcome by the brilliant daylight of those suns which once were Eva's eyes in the "dream of love." In other words, art as supreme value is the noblest of illusions and is now triumphant over the supreme value of the *Liebestraum;* for Walter's Eva in Paradise is beheld at last united with the Muse of Art—"Parnass *und* Paradies":

> Huldreichster Tag
> dem ich aus Dichters Traum erwacht:
> Das ich geträumt, das Paradies,
> in himmlisch neu verklärter Pracht
> hell vor mir lag,
> dahin der Quell lachend mich wies:
> die, dort geboren,
> mein Herz erkoren,
> der Erde lieblichstes Bild,
> zur Muse mir geweiht,
> so heilig hehr als mild
> ward kühn von mir gefreit,
> am lichten Tag der Sonnen
> durch Sanges Sieg gewonnen
> Parnass und Paradies!

What Wagner is telling us at the conclusion of Walter's Prize Song is that the return to Paradise makes it in fact a *new* Paradise when Parnassus absorbs it by means of the noble fiction of art. Or, looked at in a slightly different way, Paradise, as a realm of total value based on tradition and faith, is supplanted by art as the primary source of value, the authority for which is merely the conscious volition of the creative genius, who may employ the idea of "Paradise" as supreme fiction. Yet Walter's Paradise is not only the world of pure value of Christian mythology; it is also a realm of unalloyed eroticism, in which Eva resides. Therefore, Wagner's Paradise symbol has a double edge. Like Parnassus and erotic love, Paradise is an illusion that may be controlled and exploited by art, which claims, just as Wagner says, to be nothing but illusion.

Eva stays in Paradise only as long as Walter wants to keep her there. Walter, in other words, learns to do what Wagner and Hans Sachs have been doing throughout the drama by using the familiar and venerable myths of baptism, Paradise, and love, as supreme fictions.

Standing above illusion, the shoemaker-poet is in a position to choose and manipulate at will any illusion of the people, as well as the artistic illusions sacred to the Mastersingers and their *Tabulatur*. Hans Sachs knows what, a generation later, Ibsen's Dr. Relling tells us in *The Wild Duck* (1884), namely, that "if you take away illusion from the average man, you rob him of his happiness at the same stroke" (V,2).[8] For the same reason, Hans Sachs now chides Walter for disclaiming the whole tradition and authority of the Masters. For winning the contest, Pogner presents Walter with the hand of his daughter Eva, as well as with the image of King David on a golden chain; but the knight will not accept this emblem of masterhood. "Not a Master! No!" Walter exclaims. "I want to find happiness without Masters!"

Hans Sachs gravely urges Walter not to disparage the Masters and their art. Sachs means that Walter must now learn to become a shoemaker in his own right; he must learn to live *in* the world of *Wahn* at least, if not *by* it. Nor should he disclaim the illusions of the community in general, or their faith in "German" art. These sustain the folk, just as the artist guides the illusions toward nobler ends. Richard Wagner is telling us through Hans Sachs that the individual's genius becomes meaningful solely as it is integrated with the community, and that the artist's salvation becomes significant only if he manages to introduce novel value into society via its sacred illusions; just as Wagner does in this work and in the one to follow, and as Walter does when he renews Paradise by uniting it with Parnassus. The problem of re-entry, posed as far back as *The Flying Dutchman*, has been resolved.

Yet the solution of *Die Meistersinger* is a tentative one at best; it does not extend far enough. For Walter's regeneration of art in the evolution of his Prize Song extends only to the special community of the Mastersingers, who are themselves artists and, consequently, comprise a rather esoteric group in respect to society at large. It is noteworthy that after Walter sings his imposing song, the people enthusiastically voice their admiration by describing how they were "lulled by the loveliest dream." They heard it clearly enough, they announce; yet they scarcely fathomed it at all. Art, Wagner implies, remains for the folk only an illusion, a beautiful dream that can be grasped by faith alone, much in the way in which religion is grasped. That is the entire point. For Wagner, art may indeed function as a religion; or, seen from another angle, religion—and erotic love—function most adequately in the service of art. In other words, Wagner knows that people will go on accepting his own works in much the same spirit as the people of Nuremberg accept Walter's innovating creativity. In *Die Meistersinger*, therefore, Wagner through Hans Sachs introduces creative—and regenerating—value into the community by means of its notions about religion and love. At the end, the tradition and sacredness of these illusions remain fully intact, just as do those of Walter and Eva. In *Parsifal*, on the other hand, Wagner moves off the stage down to the orchestra pit and right into the theater itself by attempting to control (not without success) those same illusions in his captive audience.

In *Die Meistersinger*, however, the problem of illusion is answered only in part. As we have observed, Hans Sachs gains detachment from illusions, and the complete freedom to choose whichever ones he likes, solely in his own particular case. He hardly sets an example for other people, except for Walter. Yet Walter, in the end, does not become a Sachs. Ultimately, his illusions, together with those of the Nuremberg populace, are manipulated on the same strings by a shoemaker who tacitly, and a little reluctantly perhaps, plays God. At the end, Walter von Stolzing has not sufficiently released himself from the necessity for illusion to be able to locate it wherever it appears, whether in himself or others. There are some intimations that he might one day learn to identify and select illusions in the mode of Hans Sachs; but of that we cannot be certain. In *Parsifal*, nonetheless, Wagner puts to audacious use every lesson he has learned in *Die Meistersinger*.

CHAPTER 6

Christianity Redeemed

IN August, 1865, scarcely a few months after the first production of *Tristan* in Munich, Wagner finished, in a matter of three days, the complete scenario for *Parsifal*. Actually, he had pondered the outline of this work since 1845, the year he first encountered Simrock's translation of Wolfram von Eschenbach's prodigious medieval epic *Parzifal*. Its lengthy gestation in Wagner's mind accounts for the speed with which the ultimate version was conceived.

It is not by chance that the *Parsifal* poem in its final form of 1877 differs but slightly from the rather short sketch set down in 1865. For in August, 1865, with the initial performance of the "unperformable" *Tristan* behind him and the composition of *Die Meistersinger* already far progressed, Wagner at last was in a position to survey as if from a mountain summit the evolution of all his work up to that time. Thoroughly aware that *Parsifal* was to be his last work and artistic testament—he had in mind no further works for the stage—Wagner could view himself standing at the pinnacle where the train of thinking he had begun with *The Flying Dutchman* was to culminate.

In July and August, 1882, barely six months before his own death, Wagner directed the first performances of his final work at the Bayreuth Festspielhaus, which had been inaugurated, we recall, with the *Ring* in 1876. To the audiences at those initial sixteen performances, *Parsifal* appeared to be—as it still does—a profound drama of Christianity played out against a traditional religious background and using generally familiar artifacts of faith. The drama bore, moreover, a subtitle that lent a certain credence to its "sacredness." Wagner designated his work as a *Bühnenweihfestspiel*, by which he intended a "festival drama for the consecration of the stage" at Bayreuth alone. That is to say, Wagner, like subsequently his widow Cosima, intended the work to be performed nowhere else. It was to remain the exclusive property of Bayreuth and the Wagner family for fifty years at least. Cosima Wagner became, therefore, thoroughly dismayed when the opera was produced, for the first time beyond Bayreuth, at the Metropolitan Opera House in New York in 1903, and on Christmas Eve at that.

What Wagner's designation of his drama actually meant to him may be fathomed partly from his own explanation of its title, set forth in a letter of 1880 written to Ludwig II of Bavaria. "How," he asks the King, "can a drama in which the most sublime mysteries of Christian faith are shown on a public stage be presented in theaters such as ours, as part of an operatic repertory and before a public such as we have? I would actually not hold it against our church authorities if they took objection, and very legitimately, to stage presentations of the holiest mysteries on those same boards which see the frivolities of yesterday and tomorrow. In full consciousness of this, I have entitled *Parsifal* a *Bühnenweihfestspiel*. I must, therefore, have a stage to dedicate to it, and this can only be my unique theater at Bayreuth. There, and there alone, shall *Parsifal* be performed in perpetuity." [1]

Such was the master's grand fiat, spurned now for generations by nearly every major opera house in the world; but scarcely with much discernment. An aura of true faith in Wagner's explicit design for Bayreuth's "consecrated stage" persists, incongruously and uncomprehendingly, abetted certainly by the halo of Christian feeling that can be seen to hover above the whole work. This is apparent from the fact that the majority of *Parsifal* productions have occurred as close to the Easter season as possible, if not on Christmas Eve. None of this makes any sense. But in the end the fault is really Wagner's. For despite the hallowed subtitle, and all of the exquisite attention he has lavished—both musically and dramatically—on its many "Christian" details, Wagner's religious world is a fake. Which is not a weakness; it rather proves to be its major strength.

Parsifal is actually another Wagnerian myth—the ultimate one —of the kind he had been conceiving ever since he juxtaposed the Tannhäuser legend with historical details of the Wartburg contest. As the crowning mythology of his career, *Parsifal* is also the most exasperatingly complete one; a giant metaphorical web held together and enlivened by a sleight-of-hand which is so ingenious that even a suggestion that all is not really what it seems to be offends the hearts of devout Wagnerians.

In spite of its mystifying surface and Wagner's careful elucidations of its subtitle to Ludwig II, the work has as little to do with "the holiest mysteries" of traditional Christianity as *Die Meistersinger* has to do with the town of Nuremberg. In reality, however, *Parsifal* may be viewed as a continuation of the latter. We will see that the notion of baptism is evolved from *Die Meistersinger* directly into the drama Wagner conceived after it. The idea of illusion, moreover, continues to be coped with. Yet the most significant development occurs in the evolution of the protagonist, Parsifal himself; or better, in what at last develops out of a series of Wagnerian relationships, such as Siegfried–Brünnhilde and Walter–Hans Sachs.

In *Parsifal*, Wagner moves the community of Nuremberg, as it were, right into the audience chamber of his Bayreuth Festspielhaus. In other words, by the same manner in which Hans Sachs first controlled illusions, or *Wahn*, for Walter and Eva and for the Nuremberg population *on stage*, Wagner can now be seen, in turn, manipulating all of the illusions familiar to his German audiences at Bayreuth and elsewhere. These audiences, Wagner informs us through his subtitle "*Bühnenweihfestspiel*," are to be "consecrated" to novel Wagnerian illusions through the transformation of the traditional ones by means of the music and the play, which claim to be nothing but fiction. Nor is that all. By ingeniously setting his tempo and calling the tune, Wagner is able to control and direct the orientation of his audience any way he likes, precisely as Hans Sachs was able to do in Nuremberg.

If we see in Wagner's achieving a nearly total suspension of disbelief a purposeful violation of his public, that is perfectly correct; and yet it is a violation through art toward nobler Wagnerian ends, exactly in the manner of the cobbler's shoemaking. No wonder Wagner demanded that *Parsifal* be always performed in his special theater and before his specially oriented audience.

I   The Fool Instructs Himself

It may be perceived how Wagner's salient ideas evolve in a straight and uninterrupted flight from *Die Meistersinger* through *Parsifal*. The scene in Act One where Parsifal is introduced exactly parallels that early scene in *Die Meistersinger* where Walter first appears in his role of guileless simpleton and naïve artist. The young Stolzing, we remember, showed himself to be thoroughly incognizant of every traditional rule and term involving the Mastersingers' art. He was, as a consequence, totally lacking the tools with which to shape his naïve inspiration into artistic form, be it orthodox or not. It remained for Hans Sachs to mold the rough clay of the young man's inspiration into genuine and recognizable—even though novel—forms of art. In this way, the shoemaker prepares Walter for his ultimate mission: the introduction of nobler values into a traditional society, where they had never existed before.

At the outset, Parsifal's level of ignorance is even greater than Walter's. His first deed is one of utter violence and stupidity, namely, his wilful but meaningless shooting down of a harmless swan in flight, and within the sacred forest of the Holy Grail. The forest lies close by the castle of Monsalvat, its borders being protected by old Gurnemanz. The boy's violence shocks the elderly man, who questions Parsifal about the reason for his arbitrary action. "I simply shoot at anything I see flying!" the young man answers.

Gurnemanz tries to awaken in the ignorant Parsifal some feelings of compassion for the beast he has just killed, and perhaps stir in him some awareness of his own transgression. When Gurnemanz points to the bird's mutilation, Parsifal breaks his bow in two and casts the pieces away. By showing such contrition, the boy makes it clear that he has at least begun to fathom the significance of compassion. In the colloquy that ensues between the old man and the boy we discover that as yet Parsifal knows very little indeed. He is seen to be a good deal more naïve than either Siegfried or Walter was at the start. Wagner characterizes this purest of simpletons graphically in the following conversation:

> GURNEMANZ: Tell me, boy!
> Do you realize your great crime?
> PARSIFAL: I did not know it.
> GURNEMANZ: Where are you from?
> PARSIFAL: I do not know.
> GURNEMANZ: Who is your father?
> PARSIFAL: I do not know.
> GURNEMANZ: Who sent you this way?
> PARSIFAL: I do not know.

GURNEMANZ: Your name, then?
PARSIFAL: I had many,
          but I can no longer recall any of them.

With his appearance in Act One, Parsifal obviously represents unadulterated simplicity, a perfectly blank slate. That is the entire point, as Gurnemanz begins to suspect. He begins to wonder whether this dumb, but scarcely insensitive, boy might not actually fulfill the prophecy of the Holy Grail. That prophecy states that one day a guileless simpleton, "the pure fool made wise by compassion and empathy," would make himself known and save society—in this case, the sick community of the knights who guard the sacred Grail at Monsalvat.

It is quite clear how Wagner's philosophical thinking had gradually evolved up to this point. It is a development anticipated by the fearless Siegfried; yet the immediate forerunner of the important prophecy of the Grail in connection with a "pure fool" is obviously the statement made by Hans Sachs to the guild members in Act One of *Die Meistersinger*. We remember that Sachs, before he was even aware of Walter's existence, announced to the assembly of Masters that at least once every year all rules of art must be tested against time and practice, in order to judge which of them ought to be discarded or renovated. This can only be done, Hans Sachs insisted, by one who knows nothing whatsoever about the sacred *Tabulatur*. The essence of all this is recaptured early in *Parsifal*. Once again, immediately before the hero's entrance, a wise and elderly man reiterates a prophecy about a being who, in the beginning, knows nothing at all, but who learns to be wise through the insight of compassion.

At the very outset, then, Parsifal is totally ignorant. If he does not know that it is wrong to harm animals (Wagner was a leader in the German Humane Society), he also knows nothing concerning the code of ethics in the Christian society represented by Gurnemanz and the knights of the Holy Grail. In effect, he is no more aware of that community's rules about faith and salvation or its precepts of good and evil than Walter von Stolzing was aware of the mechanics and rules of art. But whereas in *Die Meistersinger* all the means of salvation are carefully manipulated by Hans Sachs, Wagner soon shows how Parsifal surpasses the role of

Sachs–Gurnemanz by manipulating the means for salvation solely by himself. In other words, he learns how to become both Sachs and Walter when he introduces new value into an outworn society by deliberately controlling and directing its dominating illusions, in the same way in which Wagner directed similar illusions in his Bayreuth audience. Wagner, we must never forget, never lets go the helm.

At this stage, Parsifal is able to reward all of Gurnemanz' queries with one single answer. Once he had a mother named Herzeleide (Sorrowing Heart). Their home was the forest and the wild meadow. This is all the dumb Parsifal can recall. But the strange woman Kundry, shouting coarsely from a thicket where she lies, offers additional information: The lad's mother bore him fatherless, for Gamuret was slain in battle. To guard her son against the same fate, Herzeleide reared the boy in isolation, ignorant of men and weapons, and brought him up a fool. "Foolish woman," Kundry adds, laughing harshly.

Kundry's narration sparks Parsifal's memory. He recalls how seeing armored men on lovely animals riding past his forest retreat, he attempted to follow them. He journeyed through wilderness day and night; his bow had to serve him against both beasts and surly men. As Kundry eagerly points out, the mortals learned to fear the fearless, terrifying boy.

Parsifal asks who was afraid of him. Evil people, the wild Kundry rejoins. Whereupon the boy demands to know whether those who threatened him were evil. Who, then, is good? Amused at this naïveté, Gurnemanz points out that Parsifal's mother from whom he ran away was good; now she weeps and suffers from Parsifal's absence. Yet the wild woman who knows so much once again gives some startling information: "Her suffering is ended— his mother is dead. I rode past and saw her as she died. To you, fool, she bade me relay greetings!"

Parsifal is enraged by Kundry's shocking report. He proceeds to grab her by the throat, but Gurnemanz stops him with the remark: "What? More violence, crazy boy? What did this poor woman ever do to you? She told the truth, for Kundry never lies, no matter how much she sees." Parsifal begins to feel faint. As she is to do later in a different context, Kundry comes to his aid. She brings him water, sprinkles some of it on his head and face and gives him the rest to drink. But she will accept no thanks for her good deed. She announces with a terrified groan that she feels deathly tired, and must sleep, must sleep.

Kundry collapses behind a bush; but Gurnemanz places his hand on Parsifal's shoulder. He tells the boy that he will lead him to the Temple of the Grail. As the two start to leave, the boy asks the old man: Who is the Grail? Gurnemanz answers that if Parsifal is truly the one the Grail has chosen, in time he will come upon its meaning. As Parsifal enters the realm of Monsalvat, Gurnemanz informs him that "here space and time are one."

The events the elderly man has just witnessed cause him to be more than hopeful that the youth by his side will indeed prove to be that "pure simpleton" whom the Grail has foreseen. Sage warden of Monsalvat's forest sanctuary and imbued with all of Christianity's codes and mores, the venerable Gurnemanz often assumes the dramatist's function. He does this when he informs the audience of past events and personal associations, just as he sometimes imparts such knowledge to the characters on stage.

Kundry, however, remains a mystery to the last. But she is Wagner's mystery. With some deliberation, he sought to preserve her cryptic aura throughout the work. She is, in fact, so mysterious that no one character on stage quite manages to figure her out, except perhaps Parsifal—and then only at the end. Yet for the viewer, Kundry appears to be relentlessly enigmatic. Her tracks remain so well covered that she can easily be viewed as one of the most complex personalities in the history of drama.

During her first encounter with Parsifal, she emerges clearly as his major adversary; yet she is also the person who understands him best of all from first to last: first as foe, but ultimately as redeemer. Already in Act One, Kundry prefigures the two major events of Parsifal's career: his confrontation with erotic love, and his final baptism. When, for example, in the first scene of Act One, she informs Parsifal that his dying mother relays through her a mother's final greeting of love, it is merely to inform him of the same episode once again—and far more meaningfully and explicitly—at the central moment of Act Two. If, on the other hand, she attempts to revive Parsifal by sprinkling him with water, after he has tried to strangle her, it seems but a preparation for a similar scene in Act Three, which is much more elaborate and significant. From the start, therefore, we grow aware of two significant trends in the relation of Kundry to Parsifal. They are trends that increase the scope of their relationship in the acts to follow: the theme of the maternal image lurking behind the mask of erotic love (a theme that is first introduced when Siegfried lays eyes on Brünnhilde), and the theme of baptism with which we are already familiar from *Die Meistersinger*. *Parsifal* can actually be seen to evolve directly out of the former work, just as its name character evolves unequivocally from Walter von Stolzing.

Unlike Parsifal, Walter is not quite a *tabula rasa* at the beginning: at least he knows that he has come to Nuremberg "because of his love for art." In other words, he seems to be conscious from the outset of some kind of personal mission in society. But in nearly all of his appearance in Act One, Parsifal clearly demonstrates that he knows nothing at all.

Both personalities, however, have a preceptor from the start; yet with an important difference. Whereas Walter remains, to the end, somewhat within the illusions directed for him and the community by Hans Sachs, Parsifal ultimately surpasses the traditional knowledge of Gurnemanz, together with the religious and social illusions of the Monsalvat community. In this fashion, he is able finally to introduce wholly novel and regenerative values into the outmoded and sick society of the Grail. Let us see how he accomplishes this.

Having demonstrated his total ignorance, Parsifal is led by Gurnemanz into the sacred confines of the Grail's abode. Here the old man tells the boy to give the closest attention to everything he is about to see. Gurnemanz thinks that only in this, if in any, way will he be able to judge whether the boy is indeed that guileless simpleton promised by the Grail.

The first thing which the boy observes in the vaulted sanctuary is the suffering Amfortas, who has charge of the Grail itself—that holy vessel from which Christ is said to have drunk at the Last Supper. The same cup also caught His blood as He hung wounded upon the Cross, pierced by the spear of Longinus. The torment of Amfortas comes from a wound struck by that same spear, for it smarts and festers but never heals in his side. (In the medieval poem, however, the wound is in the groin of the Grail's King).[2]

The sacred weapon of Longinus, along with the Grail, had for a long time played an impotrant role in Monsalvat society. But if the holy vessel remains in the keeping of Amfortas and his knights, the spear now seems irretrievably lost. Without its important companion the Grail is virtually, and paradoxically, more of a horror than a boon, at least for Amfortas. The Grail's beneficent glow continues to sustain the perception of value in the community of the knights, for which it was intended. Yet that same light merely sustains Amfortas in his agony; it keeps him only fitfully alive, like his father Titurel, who perpetually lies in his coffin, unable to expire. It is clear that for them the Grail has become a diminishing source of value.

The spear has long been abandoned to the evil hand of Klingsor, the sorcerer, who robbed it from Amfortas as he lay in Kundry's embrace in Klingsor's enchanted garden. The sorcerer then flung the weapon at the sated knight, who still bears the wound which never closes in his side, or in his groin.

Like Alberich, his villain brother beneath the skin, Klingsor has the morals and scruples of a young jaguar. Like the Nibelung, he hopes to attain supreme dominion over society; the means he uses to this end are nearly the same. In the fashion of Alberich, he has renounced love. Unlike his colleague in evil, however, the sorcerer has been compelled to renounce lust as well. For at one time—in a moment of terrifying ambition—Klingsor had emasculated himself, grimly aspiring, in this way, to coerce a holy, yet perversely guided, chastity that might befit him for his dark reign over the world of the Grail. The sorcerer thereby hopes to join the treasure of the sacred Grail to that of the lance, as a reward for his abiding erotic frustration. These two holy objects, in fact, can thus be seen to function precisely in the manner of the gold in the *Ring:* in Klingsor's hands the Grail and the spear will also turn into implements of boundless, arbitrary power.

In order to disrupt and eventually undermine all the idealized purity of Christian society, Klingsor has long stood like some giant spider in the core of a web of lust, intent on beguiling and destroying as many of the Grail's knights as he can. Kundry herself has been the enchanting but unwilling bait. Forced into whorish servitude by the master who now controls the spear, she must lure one knight after the other into her erotic trap.

Many of the Grail's loyal, chaste servants have already been ruined in this fashion. Amfortas was only the most recent and succulent prize caught in Klingsor's snare. The frightening open "wound" which Parsifal observes in the tortured Amfortas, however, is in reality the same that caused the worst sufferings of Tristan. Wagner himself was more than explicit on this cogent point. The fact that as early as 1859 the wound of Amfortas was inextricably associated with Tristan's, is clearly evident from his own remarks in a letter to Mathilde Wesendonk dated May 30 of that year. In the thick of composing Act Three of *Tristan* at Lucerne, Wagner's thoughts—astoundingly enough—turned once again to Parsifal.

Amfortas, he writes, is actually the central personage of his drama to be; and one fact, he continues, has suddenly become terribly clear to him: Amfortas "is my Tristan of the third act, but enormously intensified." [3] No comment could put Amfortas, and the entire problem of eroticism later confronted by Parsifal, in a more meaningful perspective.

Standing in motionless astonishment in the temple of the Grail, Parsifal observes the knights bearing forth the vessel which the lips of the Savior touched. The boy watches Amfortas seated before the covered shrine, unwilling to fulfill the sacred office that requires him to reveal the nourishing brilliance of the holy chalice. For if the valuable light sustains the knights, it merely prolongs and deepens the anguish of the Grail king. "The wound," Amfortas exclaims, "is nothing compared to the raging pain, the hellish need, of being condemned to this office!"

Continually observing without moving from the spot, Parsifal listens intently as the tormented man depicts the agony of the lance that pierced both Christ and himself. He hears Amfortas lament how "the Savior, with the blessed yearning of compassion, sorrows with tears of blood for the outrage of mankind's plight."

> Hier durch die Wunde, der Seinen gleich,
> geschlagen von desselben Speeres Streich,
> der dort dem Erlöser die Wunde stach,
> aus der mit blutigen Tränen
> der Göttliche weint' ob der Menschheit Schmach
> in Mitleids heiligem Sehnen, . . .

When Amfortas speaks of the agony of the Savior's torn flesh, which fills his own heart with pain, Parsifal, who has only watched and listened up to now, with a single violent motion expresses the sole apparent reaction he has to this entire scene. The boy impulsively grips his heart at the moment when he hears Amfortas mention the torment in his own. This gesture is but the outward portrayal of Parsifal's empathy with the tortured man; it is also to be taken as a sign of the stupid boy's inner development.

Watching the transmutation of the wine and the bread, which —as angelic voices proclaim from on high—were once transformed by the Lord at the Last Supper out of His compassionate love, Parsifal at the end of the Love Feast hears the boys and the knights announce how one is saved through "love and faith" (*Liebe und Glauben*).

Parsifal remains in a rigid stance as the Grail is covered and borne away; after Amfortas has departed with his knights, Gurnemanz steps up to the motionless boy and shakes him. Does he know what he has just seen? Does he grasp any of its meaning? Parsifal makes one more convulsive gesture toward his heart, but shakes his head in unrelieved ignorance. "You are still a fool, for sure," Gurnemanz comments in irritation, adding that Parsifal should depart and leave the swans in peace. If he is so stupid, the old man shouts after him, it would be far better for him to play with geese. If the guileless fool has begun to develop, he has not yet developed very far.

Even though at the beginning Parsifal showed some inkling of empathy for the animal his bow slew; and although now, in the temple of the Grail, he has shown substantially more feelings of compassion for the suffering of Amfortas, he is yet to become what the prophecy stated he must be: *durch Mitleid wissend*. That is to say, he must yet evolve into being "knowledgeable through compassion." Parsifal still does not comprehend the genuine nature of Amfortas' torment, nor can he fathom its true cause. The boy's evolution is aptly characterized by Wagner himself, in a letter of 1877, addressed to the young Judith Gautier in Paris, at about the time when he began to write the music. Wagner describes how, at the outset, Parsifal is "the foolish lad, without education or studies, who grasps things solely through compassion and empathy." [4] We have just seen how Wagner makes this clear in the course of the first act.

She-devil and whore, Kundry is caught in Klingsor's fierce but chaste grasp. Her "master" has torn her once more out of the trance-like slumber that separates her hellish existence with him from the tiresome life she leads as a messenger and household drudge for the knights of Monsalvat. In Act One, Gurnemanz informs us that Kundry exists in the present, "perhaps renewed, in order to expiate sin from a previous life that has not yet been forgiven her." This, however, is scarcely a reference to the Christian doctrine about salvation and sin that one might expect from a work whose spirit seems to be as wholly "Christian" as this one. In actuality, it is the doctrine of *karma*, which forms part of the basic ethic of both Hinduism and Buddhism. *Karma* maintains that the evil and sin of a former life may be washed away through expiation in a subsequent incarnation. Wagner obviously implies that *karma* somehow guides Kundry's destiny.[5]

No one knows where Kundry comes from, nor how old she is. Wagner permits us to infer that she has wandered from life to life. Her sins and her reincarnations may reach as far back into an ancient past as they might extend into an endless future, throughout numerous existences of ceaseless, cosmic retribution and expiation—were it not for Parsifal. He alone is able ultimately to release her from thralldom both to Klingsor and to Amfortas, and from bad *karma*.

Kundry's relationship to Amfortas is easily as profound as the terrible bond that links her to the sorcerer. In her existence as a servant of the knights of the Grail Kundry travels through the world seeking a balsam, if not a cure, for the pain of Monsalvat's wounded king. In the first act, with nearly abject devotion, she offers Amfortas a balsam from Arabia to relieve the torment she herself was instrumental in inflicting during her evil incarnation with Klingsor. Yet now as before, Kundry's aid to Amfortas proves to be in vain. Indeed, neither of them is aware of their relationship in Kundry's other life. Each of them remains oblivious to the knight's seduction and laceration at Klingsor's and Kundry's hands. In the Peters score of *Parsifal*, Wagner at this point makes a comment that lucidly reveals that fact. At the moment when Kundry refuses Amfortas' thanks for the balsam, Wagner writes above the vocal line: "Kundry has no awareness of her connection with Amfortas. This dawns on her only in the second act at [Parsifal's] words: 'If you show me the way to Amfortas'; accord-

ingly, Kundry is not supposed to be listening attentively here." [6]
The events in Klingsor's garden of lust reveal the interrelationship
of all three characters in a strong light.

With the purloined spear of Longinus in his fist, the sorcerer
stands evilly at the core of his web. Kundry is once more en-
snared, and Klingsor now summons her out of the heavy sleep
that brings her to him from her other life. She arises, shrieking,
from the ground. Klingsor's gruesome power binds Kundry in
whorish servitude, just as his magic is about to entice the pure
youth into her erotic web.

If the evil Klingsor appears to be set, in this way, in direct op-
position to the suffering Amfortas, he is in truth closely related to
the anguished man of faith: it was out of faith alone that Klingsor
committed the drastic act of self-mutilation, hoping thereby to
wrest a kind of salvation from such perversity. "I once struggled
to attain holiness," he says in this scene.

His statement also allows us to glimpse a barely visible cord
that ties Klingsor—who yearns for faith and salvation within traditional Christian limits—to Amfortas, the sick Grail king, who
also cannot achieve salvation because of "the wound," the mutilation in his groin. For this painful taint in "the side" of Amfortas
was struck by the spear now wielded by the sorcerer, who aspires
to procure with it certain mastery over the Grail itself, and thus
over all of Monsalvat society.

When we grasp the meaning of the enslavement of masculine
identity through eroticism, and its own laceration by means of the
erotic symbol of the spear, Wagner's intention becomes unmistakably clear: the spear, which is the phallus, turns into its own
enemy when it exclusively serves either eroticism or power. Thus,
if the "wound" of Amfortas functions in the same way as Tristan's
wound (and for the same reason), Klingsor's self-inflicted
"wound" enables him to exploit eroticism through the spear, and
to exploit Kundry, in order to gain power in the fashion of Alberich; it is only the more vicious, since Klingsor was forced to
renounce lust as well as love when he lacerated himself.

Now Wagner shows us, however, not the self-destructive paths
of Tristan or Alberich; he rather illustrates the annihilating nature of power and eroticism within Christian society and on its
own terms. He seems to say that both Klingsor and Amfortas are

foiled in their drive for salvation and their attempt to acquire holiness, simply because they are both fooled by their belief in the Christian illusions about power, love and lust: For both of them try to resolve the frightening Christian dilemma, its cosmic "either/or" of evil *or* good, lust *or* holiness. As Parsifal finally demonstrates, neither one nor the other can ever lead to salvation.

This crucial revelation occurs in Act Two, when Parsifal comes on stage after Klingsor has once more forced the enslaved Kundry into the role of courtesan. Klingsor now commands her to ensnare the guileless boy, just as she once did so disastrously with the ailing Amfortas. The unwitting Parsifal is to be "wounded" with the same spear that was ripped from Amfortas' grasp when he was lying in Kundry's embrace.

Klingsor informs Kundry that she will be liberated from his control only by a man who can defy her charms. He ordains that Parsifal, who approaches, will be the next to have his "innocence" tested. Kundry is utterly desperate, yet she knows that she *must* obey.

Kundry appears, preceded by the gorgeous flower maidens who envelope Parsifal with glowing attention. Klingsor has transformed her. She has become the epitome of female loveliness and now begins to entice the guileless boy. Kundry tells Parsifal that she remembers his mother well, as she held the infant child at her breast. But when as a youngster Parsifal left Herzeleide in search of wild adventure, she was driven to loneliness and sorrow, a profound sadness caused by him. The startling awareness of his former indifference now torments Parsifal to such a degree that he admits his guilt and actually accuses himself of having murdered his mother.

Kundry quickly grasps the opportunity offered by the boy's filial anguish: she pointedly assumes the guise of his second mother; or, rather, she momentarily dons the maternal mask that conceals, for a time, the image of the eternal mistress. By soothing his frayed conscience, Kundry hopes to lure Parsifal to enjoy carnal love. She begins his seduction by informing him of the sensual love which Herzeleide once had for his father Gamuret. "Just as your mother gave you life and limb," Kundry continues, "so now she brings you the first kiss of love as the final token of her mother's blessing."

> . . . die Liebe lerne kennen,
> die Gamuret umschloss,
> als Herzeleids Entbrennen
> ihn sengend überfloss:
> die Leib und Leben
> einst dir gegeben,
> der Tod und Torheit weichen muss,
> sie beut
> dir heut—
> als Muttersegens letzten Gruss
> der Liebe ersten Kuss.

Kundry's long and fervid kiss starts an agonizing metamorphosis within the boy. Suddenly it hurls him so far beyond innocence that he cries out the name of the one who was also struck by the same pain. "Amfortas!" he shrieks, glimpsing in a flash the eroticism lurking beneath the mask of motherhood.

Parsifal now visualizes the frightful image of the wound, the same terrible laceration that he once beheld during the service of the Grail in Amfortas' body, but which he now feels in his own. Parsifal himself tells us what the "wound" actually is. It is erotic desire, "the awful yearning that binds and enslaves every one of my senses." It means, in fact, *die Liebe als furchtbare Qual,* that "torment of love" which Siegfried once learned to fear and which at last destroyed him, just as it guided the destinies of Brünnhilde, as well as Tristan and Isolde, to destruction.

> Hier! Hier im Herzen der Brand!
> Das Sehnen, das furchtbare Sehnen,
> das alle Sinne mir fasst und zwingt!
> Oh!—Qual der Liebe—

Sex is here not yet perceived as "sin" in terms of traditional Christianity; it rather signals Parsifal's initial perception of eroticism as a bondage of torment deserving compassion. It is evident that the "wound" of Amfortas was clearly synonymous with Tristan's unclosed lesion already during Wagner's *Tristan* period. Much earlier, towards the end of 1854 when *Tristan* was first taking shape, his ever evolving imagination had struck upon the idea of bringing Parsifal, in his quest for the Grail, to Tristan's sickbed. Suffering from his wound, yet unable to die, Tristan had also become identified in Wagner's mind with the pain-wracked Amfortas, as we know. At this juncture in the composer's early thinking on the perplexing subject, Parsifal and Amfortas were somehow inextricably connected. Wagner describes his plan as follows:

I introduced an episode which I did not work out later—Parzifal, in his quest for the Grail, coming to the sick-bed of Tristan: for Tristan, ill from his wound and unable to die, had become identified in my mind with Amfortas in the Grail legend.[7]

In 1886, Hans von Wolzogen, who was a close acquaintance in the composer's later years, wrote the following account of his conversations with Wagner about this scene:

Parzifal, questing for the Grail, was to come in the course of his pilgrimage to Kareol, and there find Tristan lying on his death-bed, love-racked and despairing. Thus the longing one was brought face to face with the renouncing one, the self-curser with the man atoning for his own guilt, the one suffering unto death from love with the one bringing redemption through compassion. Here death, there new life. And it was intended that a melody associated with the wandering Parzifal should sound in the ears of the mortally wounded Tristan, as it were the mysteriously faint, receding answer to his life-destroying question about the "Why?" of life. Out of this melody, it may be said, grew the stage-festival-drama [*Parsifal*].[8]

What is evident from Wagner's original plan of 1854, as well as from Von Wolzogen's important elucidations which derive ostensibly from Wagner's own lips, is that by the mid-1850's the dramatist had already begun to see that the problem of redemption *from* love in *Tristan* was at last to be resolved through the notion of redemption *by* compassion. Nevertheless, there was to be a lapse of ten years more before Wagner, with *Tristan* completed and the problems of *Die Meistersinger* solved, could see his way clear. For by 1865, as we have already noted, Wagner had solved the question of the redemption from love by completing the full sketch for *Parsifal*. In that drama, but particularly in the confrontation of Parsifal and Kundry here under discussion, he offers the ultimate resolution.

It has taken stagefuls of dead heroes and heroines to pay for the insight which Parsifal now gains. At this moment, the perceiving boy is suddenly able to link the agony of Amfortas—which he had silently observed throughout the Grail scene—with the pain and blood of the Savior Himself. Parsifal begins to fathom far more than the "sex as sin" concept of Christian tradition. Associating the torment of Amfortas with his own, he begins to see the reason for all torment as lying not just in erotic yearning, but in the very fact of human existence, in the painful error of life itself. Only now does he understand the true meaning of the Grail king's words about the Savior, who "in the blessed yearning of compassion sorrows with tears of blood for the outrage of the human plight."

By slowly perceiving that his own "wound" stems from the same cause as those of Amfortas and the Savior on the Cross, whose wound bled for man's tragic predicament, Parsifal, through total compassion with world suffering, becomes himself the world redeemer. Yet he actually redeems no one: he only *knows*. Others may be redeemed solely by seeing, and then pursuing, the example of Parsifal's perception of the world. This is exactly what Parsifal means when he informs Kundry that *she* will be saved too, if she shows him the path back to Amfortas.

In his terrible anguish following Kundry's "kiss of love," Parsifal envisions the sacred vessel of the Grail filled with glowing blood, and he feels within himself the Savior's pain at the desecration of the Grail sanctuary. He would condemn himself for not having fully comprehended the significance of all that he beheld in the temple of the Grail. But Kundry, hoping once more to ingratiate herself, encourages Parsifal to abandon his self-accusations. By encircling him with caresses and smiles, she hopes to accomplish this. But this time Parsifal knows her game. He describes to himself every movement of her body, her face, and hands, as though he were in Amfortas' fatal place on a day long ago; now he is able to visualize the kiss which Kundry just gave him as the very kiss that once robbed Amfortas of his salvation. That is why he violently repulses the destructive enchantress.

By now we know why Parsifal must do so. His initial contrition and subsequent empathy at the sight of the harmless, dead swan victimized by his bow, followed by his intense compassion and suffering as he stood watching the agony of Amfortas in the temple of the Grail, have led Parsifal to this angry moment: to his furious rejection of Kundry out of supreme insight into the kind of torment she brings. Wagner clearly indicates to what extent in this scene and before, Parsifal actually perceives the physical anguish of the Grail king as his very own. He does this by carefully revealing each new level of Parsifal's *Entwicklung* in the acquisition of empathy. For the same reason that he smashed his dangerous bow, Parsifal later clutches at his heart while listening to the lamentations of Amfortas. Shortly before the moment in Act Two when Parsifal recalls the glowing blood in the Grail after Kundry's kiss, Wagner enters the following comment above the vocal line: "Parsifal is exactly in the state in which he had seen Amfortas." [9]

At this moment, then, Parsifal has not only been thoroughly purged of his guileless simplemindedness, but he has finally learned to feel the pain of others completely as his. Kundry, who remains Parsifal's vivid dramatic foil throughout this scene, is fully aware of this.

She now angrily reproaches him because he "feels solely the pain of others." She challenges Parsifal to perceive hers too: "If you *are* indeed a savior, what prevents you, evil man, from uniting yourself with me for *my* salvation?"

> Fühlst du im Herzen
> nur anderer Schmerzen,
> so fühle jetzt auch die meinen.
> Bist du Erlöser,
> was bannt dich, Böser,
> nicht mir auch zum Heil dich zu einen?

The type of salvation Kundry is talking about is, of course, not the kind that Parsifal means. For a long time, Kundry reveals, she has been awaiting the Savior, Him whom she once reviled with laughter while He was carrying the Cross. Scorned and rejected by her, the Redeemer's visage pursues her from life to life (thus Wagner combines the traditions of *karma* with those of Christianity). No sooner does she glimpse the true path of salvation—as a servant of Monsalvat—than the accursed laughter returns, so that she becomes Klingsor's helpless courtesan luring one more sinner into her erotic web.

Insinuating how she is forced into servitude both in the guise of
Monsalvat's drudging slave and the sorcerer's abject enslaver,
Kundry reveals that she has been thoroughly exploited in each
role. Whether she is forced into the role of courtesan for Klingsor
or is compelled to perform inarticulate and slavish duties like a
domestic animal and is merely a household drudge (Klingsor describes her as "a cow" of Monsalvat), Kundry explains how she is
only fulfilling the two feminine roles assigned her by unregen-
erate society. Symbolizing for Wagner a kind of unredeemed fem-
ininity, Kundry's whole existence is thus compelled to run along
tracks that the social order has always laid down. These tracks,
Wagner implies, move in a dark and ever more vicious circle.

We are scarcely bewildered, therefore, when Kundry's guise as
a penitent seeker of salvation abruptly changes into the role of the
courtesan once more. She tells Parsifal how her absolution and
salvation will be achieved *now* by being united with him for but
one hour. Parsifal replies, however, that for that single hour both
of them would be damned for eternity. He also confidently informs Kundry that he has been sent for her salvation also, but
only if she is able to turn away from *yearning* and *willing*
(*Sehnen*). "The tonic that ends your sufferings," Parsifal points
out, "cannot pour from the very fountain from which they flow:
salvation shall never be granted until this fountain within you
dries."

> Auch dir bin ich zum Heil gesandt,
> bleibst du dem Sehnen abgewandt.
> Die Labung, die dein Leiden endet,
> beut nicht der Quell, aus dem es fliesst:
> das Heil wird nimmer dir gespendet,
> wenn jener Quell sich dir nicht schliesst.

Now Parsifal digs out the marrow of his argument. "It is another salvation," he adds, "another kind indeed, for which I beheld such anguish; in their hideous need the Grail brethren tor-
ture and mortify the flesh because of it."

> Ein andres ist's, ein andres, ach!
> nach dem ich jammernd schmachten sah,
> die Brüder dort in grausen Nöten
> den Leib sich quälen und ertöten.

The road to true redemption, Wagner suggests, lies along wholly different paths from the one pursued by both Kundry *and* the Grail community. Neither of the ways followed by them leads anywhere but straight back to the Will, to a hot and ceaseless circuit of desiring and willing. The final implication that the direction of both paths is exactly alike is inescapable. The severe asceticism motivating the society of the Grail and its "positive" values of self-denial and self-mortification are inferred to be, in the end, as frustrating and pointless to the senses as all of Kundry's thralldom. In Wagner's view both directions merely confirm the Will's tyranny, because each of them remains inevitably tied to the ever sensing, desiring Will: they are shown, in fact, to be only different aspects of the same thing.

In other words, the polar opposites of sense desiring and sense denial, of *Lust* and *Askese*, which, for Tannhäuser, meant the alternative between Venus and Elisabeth, can actually never be resolved. For each polar end derives from the very same source: the Will, which is blind. This is why Parsifal's insight now illuminates the predicament of Christian society with a searing brilliance. He sees just how the terrible self-castigations of the Grail brotherhood, and the fact of the Grail king's painful wound, affirm the existence of the yearning Will fully as much as do the erotic hells of Kundry and Klingsor.

It is the profound knowledge of this fact that impels Wagner's protagonist to voice with such urgency the single question: "But who recognizes in perfect clarity *the only genuine source of salvation?*"

> Doch wer erkennt ihn klar und hell,
> des einz'gen Heiles wahren Quell?

Furthermore, it is madness and "blind world illusion," Parsifal adds, to be ardently in search of salvation while continuing, all along, to yearn for damnation's very source.

> Oh, Elend! Aller Rettung Flucht!
> Oh, Weltenwahns Umnachten:
> in höchsten Heiles heisser Sucht
> nach der Verdammnis Quell zu schmachten!

In rejecting asceticism *as well as* the senses as a solution to the Romantic problem of redemption, or the experience of value, Richard Wagner ostensibly contemplates a third solution, which is in no way a synthesis of the other two. Precisely what he intends as an answer to the problem of value may be fathomed only after a discussion of the events in Act Three. At this point, it is sufficient to realize that at no time before in his dramatic works had Wagner moved so far beyond his customary objectivity toward the stage action. In Parsifal's lines above, Wagner interjects a personal and philosophical guideline directly into the flow of the action. He appears indeed to have become well aware of it.

In his book *Richard Wagner: His Work and His World,* Curt von Westernhagen quotes a remark by the composer made specifically in view of these lines, a statement purportedly found in one of the diaries kept by Cosima. According to this diary, Wagner told his wife during the composition of this passage in the summer of 1878: "Very peculiar. I have never gone so far. This goes beyond the limits of the permissible into the didactic." [10]

Wagner spoke the truth; the exposition of the Wagnerian idea in the latter portion of this act takes place in a distinctly premeditated manner, much more so than even Hans Sachs's speech on *Wahn,* with its intended message. One could say that the philosophy nearly runs away with the dramatic events, were it not for the fact that the music goes a long way toward making things artistically acceptable.

Now the complicated weave unwinds. Kundry asks—with ironic effect—if it was not her kiss that gave Parsifal universal insight. She exclaims that her passionate embrace led him to attain divinity and bitterly remarks that he should go on to redeem the world if that is his calling. But the very hour that made him a redeemer also leaves her eternally damned.

> So war es mein Kuss,
> der welthellsichtig dich machte?
> mein volles Liebesumfangen
> lässt dich dann Gottheit erlangen!
> Die Welt erlöse, ist dies dein Amt:
> schuf dich zum Gott die Stunde,
> für sie lasse mich ewig verdammt,
> nie heile mir die Wunde.

It is perfectly apparent how, through his total compassion and his selfless perception of suffering existence, Parsifal has become a divinity in his own right—according to Wagner, if not according to Christian tradition. It is Parsifal's complete empathy with the suffering human condition—in fact with the very condition of all life—that makes him so. In his pervasive view, Parsifal—as well as Wagner—beholds "sin" not as a cause but as a symptom; for both the erotic yearning of the Will and man's attempt to mortify it through asceticism are sinful in the Wagnerian lexicon, since each reveals the same cause. That both ways are equally spurious in achieving any kind of salvation is now made explicit.

Replying to Kundry's bitter remarks, Parsifal announces that he offers her salvation also. Yet Kundry, still incorrigible, persists in her previous demand that Parsifal bring her redemption through an hour of love. Now, the true meaning of Parsifal's attitude dawns upon the attentive Kundry. "Love and deliverance shall be yours too," Parsifal advises her (Wagner notes above the vocal line that "Kundry is listening carefully," and that "this is the turning-point of all events."), "if you show me the way to Amfortas."

> Lieb' und Erlösung soll dir werden,—
> (*Kundry gespannt zuhörend. Hier ist*
> *der Wendepunkt der ganzen Entwicklung.*)
> zeigest du
> zu Amfortas mir den Weg.

Wagner's insistence on the fact that Kundry listens intently to Parsifal's promise of salvation *if* she shows him the way back to Amfortas, and that this contingency signals a crucial point of change in the dramatic events, is not a sudden afterthought on Wagner's part. Parsifal's statement had been carefully prepared during the first scene of Act One. There, when Amfortas is borne in on a litter on his way to seek relief from his pain, Kundry rushes forth with a special balsam, which she has brought from Arabia on her endless travels in the service of the Grail. Yet no one, Kundry least of all, is aware of the cryptic relationship which links her with the chaste brotherhood and its suffering king in a role of enslaved whore to Klingsor. For this reason, when Amfortas beckons to Kundry in order to thank her for her trouble, she remains lying on the ground and refuses to acknowledge his grati-

tude. Wagner's comment in the score, we recall, establishes a connection between this situation and the occurrence in Act Two.
Wagner says: "Kundry has no awareness of her relation to Amfortas. This dawns on her only in Act Two at the words: 'If you
show me the way to Amfortas'; that is why Kundry is not supposed
to be listening attentively here." [11]

This means that, as Parsifal informs her, Kundry's complete release now depends on her gaining insight that it was she who
caused Amfortas' wound in the first place. If Kundry can cast off
her role through an inkling of compassion sufficient to direct Parsifal to the anguished Amfortas, then she will be filled with a
sense of empathy for world suffering, and she will find her *own*
redemption.

Rather than achieving insight, Kundry merely grows furious.
She mocks Parsifal by exclaiming that he shall never find his
path to Amfortas. She rejects "the honor of his compassion" by
calling for the spear to be turned against him. Only if Parsifal
grants her one erotic hour shall he be guided on his way. But the
new savior vehemently repulses Kundry for the last time. Cursing
him, and screaming that he will never find his way out of her web,
Kundry calls for the holy spear, now in Klingsor's hand, to be
hurled against Parsifal's head.

The summoned Klingsor mounts the castle wall, and with the
poised and deadly lance hovers above Parsifal. He aims the
weapon at the boy, but it stops miraculously in mid-air above
him. Grasping the spear, Parsifal confidently swings it into the
sign of the Redeemer's passion: the Cross. He proclaims that the
power of the spear which caused the wound, shall close it also.
The deceptive splendor of Klingsor's enchanted garden, Parsifal
concludes, will now turn back into the desert wilderness that it
really is. After tumbling to the ground amid all the desolation of
the illusory garden, Kundry slowly lifts her head, glimpsing the
departing youth. From the distance she listens to his meaningful
words: "You know—," Parsifal concludes, "where you can find me
next!"

II *The Redeemer Self-Redeemed*

Unlike Kundry, Klingsor, or Amfortas, the young Parsifal—
fool no more—firmly controls the spear, simply because he is no
longer controlled by its eroticism. His possessing the weapon

signalizes his power over himself, and this becomes the most significant event along the path of his self-instruction. At this stage in his development, Parsifal has withstood and opposed both the tyranny and the castigation of the senses, since he has gradually pierced the illusions that pertain to each. He also therefore transcends—just as we have perceived in his scene with Kundry—the illusions of the typical male role. Kundry herself is perfectly aware of this, as she makes clear near the end of the long scene with Parsifal, even though she convinces us of her perception of the youth's total self-mastery only in her bitterly ironic comment about his being "the redeemer." But Kundry's negative attitude does not alter the facts. In Act Three, we obtain for the first time a keenly etched portrait of the new kind of savior. There now emerges the Wagnerian redeemer who redeems himself.

At the outset of the final act, Gurnemanz discovers Kundry, almost lifeless, groaning in a thicket. She has once more taken on her role of cow-like servant to the Grail society. Significantly, however, she is this time described as having lost her former wildness. She is no longer a thrall to "bad *karma*," which in a dual role has driven her relentlessly throughout the centuries. Rather, she has gained complete humility. Appropriately, Kundry's only words in this act are: "Let me serve . . . serve!"

Carrying the recovered spear, Parsifal soon enters the forested meadowland. He is attired wholly in black armor, which, for a time, conceals his identity even from Gurnemanz. The elderly man asks the odd-looking warrior whether he has been among the heathen: does the stranger fail to realize that today is Good Friday, a time when no mortal bears armor or weapons of any kind? The silent boy shakes his head in ignorance. Beholding this, Gurnemanz reprimands Parsifal for his stupidity and orders him to remove his warlike garments. Gurnemanz admonishes the stranger that he, as a proper Christian, should be mindful that on this day the Lord shed His holy blood for the sake of the sinful world.

Remaining silent, Parsifal plunges the end of the spear into the ground and lays his shield and sword down next to it. Then, opening his black visor, he lifts his helmet off and places it beside his weapons. Parsifal now sinks down in silent prayer before the lance. The old man observes him with mounting astonishment and emotion, for he suddenly recalls the simpleton who, long ago, slew the swan—the very boy, he recollects, whom he once rudely cast out of the temple of the Grail.

Deeply stirred, Gurnemanz also recognizes the spear, to whose point the kneeling Parsifal ardently raises his own eyes. The young man expresses his joy at finding Gurnemanz once again. To the elderly man's questioning about where he has been, Parsifal replies that he was led along paths of error and suffering.

Gurnemanz asks him where he is going. "To *him*," Parsifal answers, "whose profound anguish I once perceived in foolish silence, but to whom now I consider myself to be chosen to bring salvation."

> Zu ihm, des tiefe Klagen
> ich törig staunend einst vernahm,
> dem nun ich Heil zu bringen
> mich auserlesen wähnen darf.

Until now, Parsifal goes on to say, he has been unable to behold the road to salvation. A horrendous curse drove him about in every direction on paths of error. Hardships without number, battles and conflicts, forced him off the path at times when he was sure that he had just found its true course. In spite of all, Parsifal joyfully announces, he has managed to bring home the sacred lance at last.

In this way, Wagner suggests that the spear is a symbol of value for a moribund society. Because this society has become outworn, its values are no longer pertinent. It is quite apparent, moreover, that Christian society in the nineteenth century, as Wagner saw it, faced the same predicament.

Gurnemanz vividly details the Grail brethren's deplorable state of affairs. He describes how the knights are eagerly awaiting Parsifal's return with the spear, for to them the recovery of the weapon betokens a salvation which they sorely need. Things are presently so moribund at Monsalvat, moreover, that Amfortas himself, yearning continually for death to end his torment, has lately refused even to uncover the Grail. He hopes that, deprived of its nourishing light, he will be allowed to perish from his anguishing wound. By the same token, all of his knights, deprived of the nourishing glow, are succumbing to a general spiritual malaise.

Without the miraculous light, Titurel, the father of Amfortas, has already died. Engulfed by starvation, Amfortas is growing ever weaker; but he cannot die. Yet, no amount of entreaty by the brethren can induce him to reveal the brilliance of the vessel once more. Amfortas completely refuses to perform the duties of the holy office.

On account of this widespread deterioration, no summonses have been coming from far lands for the knights to journey forth to battle for the faith. Abjectly miserable and ill, Grail society drifts about spiritlessly and without leadership. Parsifal blames himself and his past ignorance for all this waste and chaos. The young man is suddenly overcome by such feelings of culpability that he almost swoons. But Gurnemanz comes to his aid, and Kundry fetches water to refresh him.

The idea of baptism, so familiar from *Die Meistersinger*—and of such significance there—is introduced once again. Waving Kundry's help aside, Gurnemanz proclaims that the waters of the holy fount itself are needed to wash away all the dust and error from Parsifal's head. Gurnemanz also foretells how Parsifal, once consecrated, is yet to perform—on that very day—a mighty task: he will re-establish the sacred office of the Holy Grail.

Kundry portrays the very archetype of Christian humility when she kneels now to wash the feet of the chosen one. Observing her with astonishment, Parsifal remarks that just as Kundry "has bathed my feet, so let friend Gurnemanz now moisten my crown." Dipping his hand into the fount, Gurnemanz anoints the youth, saying, in the manner of a ritual, that "the pure being shall be blessed through purity." The apparent sanctity of this moment is enhanced by another cryptic Wagnerian message, written above the vocal line of the score: "What transpires between them all remains a tremendous enigma; one cannot tell whether Parsifal recognizes Kundry or not." [12]

While Gurnemanz anoints the young man's head, Kundry pours the contents of a golden flask over his feet and—recalling the repentant Maria Magdalene—dries them with her long, unbound hair. It is during this deed of penance and humility that Parsifal gradually recognizes who Kundry really is. His whole development is clearly complete at the moment when he takes the flask from Kundry's hands, gives it to Gurnemanz, and announces with "an expression that is increasingly proud": "You anointed my

feet; let Titurel's companion now anoint my head, so that even on
this day he may greet me as a king,"

> Du salbtest mir die Füsse,
> (*Mit gesteigert stolzem Ausdruck*)
> das Haupt nun salbe Titurels Genoss,
> (*gross, befehlend*)
> dass heute noch als König er mich grüsse.

It can be seen that whereas Hans Sachs, unilaterally assuming the role of his namesake John the Baptist, anointed Walter's new song for a novel task, Parsifal, who may be viewed as a
continuation of Walter, here *commands his own mentor to baptize him*. In other words, if Gurnemanz, up to now, has performed
the role of John the Baptist, Parsifal learns to intercept the old
man in his role and to become the Baptizer himself. By doing this,
Parsifal shows that he has grown to perceive the nature of illusion
and, having penetrated its veils, has learned to manipulate it precisely as Hans Sachs does.

That is to say, Parsifal has at last grown fully conscious of the
need for his appearance as a new Christ in the society of Monsalvat. He therefore *must appear* to be symbolically consecrated—
not only to Kundry, Gurnemanz, and the brethren of the Grail,
but to Wagner's special Bayreuth public as well. For if Parsifal is
indeed manipulating the Christian tradition and its illusions in the
minds of the characters on stage, Wagner himself operates in exactly the same fashion upon all the traditional feelings of his captive audience at the play, the *Bühnenweihfestspiel*. Those who
suspect a kind of trick are absolutely correct. All along, Wagner
has carefully manipulated the Christian orientations of the happily credulous public.

What this ultimately amounts to is "a festival drama" that turns
into a kind of mass, and the Bayreuth audience into a Wagnerian
congregation, while Richard Wagner himself becomes the master
preacher and master priest. It is at this juncture that the illusion
of a new Christ, which Wagner is creating, merges painlessly into
the traditional religious one of a Christian public. It is under-
standable why Wagner so adamantly insisted that *Parsifal* be performed by no other theater except his own.

Ordered by Parsifal to baptize him, Gurnemanz utters words

which are scarcely a formula for an orthodox anointing. He calls the young man "merciful through compassion" (*mitleidvoll Duldender*) and also "the one who brings salvation through knowledge" (*heiltatvoll Wissender*). Parsifal is knowledgeable at last; he is *wissend* in a fashion that Siegfried and Brünnhilde, Tristan and Isolde, or even Walter von Stolzing, could never have been; for he has become gradually insightful through the penetration of illusion and, finally, through long experiences of empathy. But if Parsifal can be seen as an ultimate fulfillment of Walter and Hans Sachs, he may also be viewed as the embodiment of Brünnhilde's final insights.

The next lines seem to be obscure. After baptizing Parsifal, Gurnemanz tells him that "just as you have suffered all the sorrows of the redeemed Christ, so now you shall raise the last burden from His head."

Wie des Erlösten Leiden du gelitten,
die letzte Last entnimm nun seinem Haupt.

It is quite likely that Wagner is telling us not only how Parsifal symbolizes Christ, but in addition—and here is the key point—that having now redeemed himself by insight and empathy, he symbolizes a Christ who *does not have to die,* but who lives.

We have the quintessence of Wagner's essentially unorthodox Christianity. Wagner reveals that here is a savior who does not take on the world's sins and then suffers death in order to redeem man from them. Parsifal redeems no one except himself. Instead of perishing in the flesh, he is saved in the flesh right here on earth, *alive.* Parsifal, all by himself, redeems himself, and others may be redeemed by following his example.

Wagner is telling us that man can be saved and that he may perceive a sense of ultimate value, if he can experience what Parsifal does. That is all, but it is enough. Only the activity stimulated by the destruction of illusion, together with empathy for the plight of all existence, becomes the ultimately meaningful experience in the social bond. But there is a corollary: illusions are necessary, as Hans Sachs knew and Parsifal knows now. But by the very act of seeing their necessity, man is freed of them and learns how to control their forces. As Morse Peckham puts it, within Parsifal "identity and value are achieved at the moment of empathy and insight. The two psychic acts are simultaneous. The problem of egocentricity does not arise, for egocentricity is the consequence of believing illusions. Egocentricity is the character of the Christian Amfortas, wounded by his surrender of identity to the illusions of religion and love." [13] It should be added that both Kundry and Klingsor surrender their identities to the same illusions.

Soon after he tells Gurnemanz to baptize him, Parsifal proves how he has learned to control all of illusion, for he then turns around and baptizes Kundry. In doing this, Parsifal reveals that his insight out of compassion is truly of the *active* kind. "Take baptism," he proclaims to Kundry, "and believe in the Savior" (die Taufe nimm,/und glaub' an den Erlöser). It is clearly implied that Kundry, since she may not be redeemed by compassionate insight, can accept on faith only a symbol of rebirth, which is baptism, from his hand.

Wolfgang Golther goes so far as to state that "in this baptismal scene Parsifal becomes Christ's representative in actual fact":[14] Golther, I believe, is misled here by dramatic appearances. It is patent that Wagner is using Parsifal as an archetype of the historical Christ, just as he employs Gurnemanz and Hans Sachs as archetypes of John the Baptist. But that is all. That Golther and so many others should, at this stage, perceive Parsifal as a true representative of the Savior Himself, however, is hardly astonishing. Wagner has very deftly allowed his own esoteric idea to remain concealed behind the obvious symbolism of a traditional Christianity. By employing a wealth of familiar religious detail—both on stage and in orchestral harmonies and cadences—Wagner has covered his tracks with such care that audiences are easily, and willingly, persuaded by his "Christian" sounds and scenes to believe that they are present at "the real thing."

One should never forget that Wagner is always in control of both the rabbit and the hat. He has memorized his own lessons from *Die Meistersinger* well. Above all, *Parsifal* is not religion, nor is it ethics or philosophy; it is art. If Wagner cleverly evokes religious associations in his audience by means of a deliberate stylization of liturgic music in the orchestra, as well as through the "sacred" panoply of events on stage, that is not the point. If *Parsifal*, in the words of the critic Paul Henry Lang, is "a pious fraud," that fact has nothing to do with its legitimate—and very significant—artistic merits. Lang is absolutely right when he insists that to Wagner "Christ was only a symbol," and he adds perceptively that "in order to represent his symbol artistically [Wagner] had to resort to well-known religious rites and figures, but God, the fount of every metaphysical religion, is nowhere mentioned in *Parsifal.*" [15]

In general, Lang's conclusions quite nearly match those of Peckham and myself, for he agrees that "*Parsifal* is an independent Wagnerian religion, a religion of art, essentially alien to Christianity even though the opera seems to suggest a Christian milieu with some Buddhism thrown in for good measure." [16]

When, unlike Walter von Stolzing, Parsifal surpasses the role of his mentor and baptist Gurnemanz by ordaining his own baptism, he shows how novel and regenerating value may be introduced into the community. Parsifal's symbolic rebirth through baptism merely serves as an example for the moribund society of Monsalvat. His baptism of Kundry and, later, his healing of Amfortas' wound figure as acts of compassion which the tormented beings accept on faith. Yet Parsifal cannot save *them*. He can save no one, because he has no transcendental authority whatever to do so. Redemption, Wagner insinuates, means to follow Parsifal's lucid example—if you can. For he is self-redeemed.

Parsifal's steps lead now in only one direction: back to Amfortas, in order to seal his wound and ultimately to juxtapose the recovered lance with a rejuvenated Grail in a nobler and wiser union. But first, the young man must learn from Gurnemanz about the anguish of Good Friday, the black Christian day which precedes the moment of "resurrection." That is to say, Wagner, through Gurnemanz, exploits the Christian dogma and ritual of death and resurrection in order to affirm his own doctrine of salvation. It is this portion of the drama that Paul Henry Lang ostensibly refers to when he thinks of *Parsifal* as "an independent Wagnerian religion."

When Parsifal exclaims that he has never seen nature in such glowing loveliness, Gurnemanz replies that he is beholding the enchantment of Good Friday. This knowledge, however, causes the youth to burst out that this is indeed the day of greatest woe: "All that blossoms, breathes, lives, and lives again," Parsifal laments, "should only mourn and weep."

> O wehe, des höchsten Schmerzentags!
> Da sollte, wähn' ich, was da blüht,
> was atmet, lebt und wieder lebt,
> nur trauern, ach! und weinen!

But Gurnemanz replies that this is not so, as he can see for himself. On this day, in fact, the meadows and fields are besprinkled with the dew from repentant sinners' tears, and nature glows and blooms. All creatures turn joyful, now that they perceive signs of the Savior, and dedicate their prayers to Him.

Most of this is scarcely unorthodox. But now the deeper threads and hues of the Wagnerian tabula of faith are woven together, against an indescribably lush bed of orchestral sound. As Gurnemanz explains, the Redeemer Himself upon the Cross remains unseen by creation's myriad and dumb beings: thus they glance up to redeemed man, who now feels freed from all the anguish and terror of sin through God's pure love sacrifice. The stalks and flowers of the meadow notice that the foot of man does not trample them today. The reason for this, the old man continues, is that just as the Lord, with divine forbearance, suffered for man out of compassion, so also, on this day, man compassionately spares God's dumb creatures by his gentle tread. All creatures who are mindless and without salvation (*erlösungslos*), who blossom and soon pass away without insight, are thankful, Gurnemanz concludes, for today nature itself is absolved and achieves a perfect innocence.

> Nun freut sich alle Kreatur
> auf des Erlösers holder Spur,
> will ihr Gebet ihm weihen.
> Ihn selbst am Kreuze kann sie nicht erschauen:
> da blickt sie zum erlösten Menschen auf;
> der fühlt sich frei von Sündenlast und Grauen,
> durch Gottes Liebesopfer rein und heil.
> Das merkt nun Halm und Blume auf den Auen,
> dass heut' des Menschen Fuss sie nicht zertritt,
> doch wohl, wie Gott mit himmlischer Geduld
> sich sein' erbarmt und für ihn litt,
> der Mensch auch heut' in frommer Huld
> sie schont mit sanftem Schritt.
> Das dankt dann alle Kreatur,
> was all da blüht und bald erstirbt,

da die entsündigte Natur
heut' ihren Unschuldstag erwirbt.

Here Wagner has penetrated the myths of Christian meta-
physics in order to recreate its illusions, in his own original terms,
as a reality. But in the end, it is Wagner's art which is the sole
illusion that produces any meaningful reality at all. Viewing
the matter from another stance, one could say that the salient
Christian doctrines of sin, compassion, and salvation are here
turned into a pseudo-reality out of which the dramatist is able to
direct the illusions of the public toward novel Wagnerian visions.
That is, in revealing a savior who may *live* and who does not have
to perish because "He so loved the world," Wagner deftly exposes
and inverts on its own terms a part of Christianity's main transcendental thesis. But in the end they are Wagner's terms. No
longer perceived as valid, Christianity is viewed as a moribund
mythology that may be exploited artistically in any fashion whatever, in order to provide a new myth of salvation. In the passage
of Gurnemanz cited above, and within *Parsifal* as a whole, Wagner creates a novel world, at least on a symbolic level. Its myth of
the possibility of man's regeneration can be seen as the answer to
the world's "Götterdämmerung."

Parsifal's gentle command that Kundry accept baptism from
him and cherish faith in her own redemption, becomes an expression of his empathic love, of the kind he promised Kundry once
before, on condition that she show him the path back to Amfortas.
Now Kundry weeps, and her lament is the cause of Parsifal's re-
membrance of their confrontation in Act Two. At that time, Kundry informed Parsifal that she had once mocked Christ himself
when she "saw Him—and laughed." Alluding now to that statement made in the past, Parsifal recollects that Kundry herself
once laughed at him and then withered away, just like Klingsor.
Parsifal inquires whether "they are eager for salvation now." Kundry's penitent tears, Parsifal comfortingly continues, have become
the blessed dew on the meadows of Good Friday. "You are weep-
ing," he tells her, "but behold the meadow, for it is smiling." Parsifal then kisses her tenderly on the brow.

Ich sah sie welken, die einst mir lachten:
ob heut sie nach Erlösung schmachten?

auch deine Träne ward zum Segenstaue:
Du weinest—sieh! es lacht die Aue.
(*Er küsst sie sanft auf die Stirne.*)

Parsifal's allusion to himself as a redeemer is too obvious to be missed. He can now be seen employing traditional beliefs much in the same way in which Hans Sachs applies the rules of the guild. Like Sachs, Parsifal has learned the meaning and function of rules in a tradition only in order to transcend them.

"Noontime," Gurnemanz announces. "The hour is here. Allow your servant, lord, to direct you on your way." Investing Parsifal with the garment of a Grail knight, the elderly man and Kundry accompany Monsalvat's new king. As the three move silently toward the temple of the Holy Grail, they are greeted by funeral bells. Entering the temple's lofty hall, Parsifal glimpses the mourning procession for the dead Titurel, whose body is carried forth in a closed coffin. The ailing Amfortas is also borne in on his sick-bed; it is lifted so that the dying king is placed before the covered shrine.

The lid of Titurel's coffin is removed before the assembly. Viewing the corpse of their one-time leader, the knights utter a cry of "Woe!" Amfortas then addresses his dead father: He yearns for his parent's spirit to intercede beyond death, so that he may be granted his own death from the agonizing wound.

"Uncover the shrine! Perform your office!" the knights clamor as they crowd about the suffering man: "Your father exhorts you! You must, you must!"

"No!" Amfortas shouts painfully. "Never again!" Plunging into the middle of his pressing colleagues, Amfortas desperately urges them to answer one question: "Is he to return to life who feels already the shapes of death gliding around him?" Amfortas rips open his garment and stands before them, exclaiming defiantly: "Take out your weapons! Bury your blades into me up to their hilts! Slay the sinner and his torment. The Grail will then surely glow for you all by itself!" With a terrible kind of ecstasy, Amfortas totters about, touching, for all to see, the bleeding laceration while swaying in pain.

Meanwhile, unperceived by the others, Parsifal has advanced to the spot. He carries the sacred lance. Extending the spear, he poises its tip against the wound of the suffering man: "Only one weapon serves," Parsifal proclaims, "The wound is closed solely by the point which struck it open."

> Nur eine Waffe taugt!
> Die Wunde schliesst
> der Speer nur, der sie schlug.

"Be healed, be absolved, and find atonement," Parsifal announces, "for I shall henceforth take your office. Your suffering is blessed," he informs Amfortas, "for having bestowed upon the timid simpleton the strength of compassion and perfect wisdom."

> Gesegnet sei dein Leiden,
> das Mitleids höchste Kraft
> und reinsten Wissens Macht
> dem zagen Toren gab.

To the entire gathering Parsifal declares that he brings back to them the holy spear. Then rejoining the spear with the Grail, he announces that the light of the vessel shall be hidden from them no more, just as the wound of Amfortas will now stay forever closed.

Opening the shrine, Parsifal takes the Grail into his own hand and raises it aloft. With ever increasing brilliance, the vessel shines forth over the community of Monsalvat. Glancing up to her redeemer, Kundry slowly expires, sinking to the ground. Amfortas, Gurnemanz, and all the knights kneel in honor of their young king.

The brotherhood of knights proclaims the miracle of salvation, announcing that "the redeemer is redeemed." Their words are soon taken up by all those present, and this ultimate proclamation of every voice is answered at last by unseen voices issuing from extreme heights of the temple:

> Höchsten Heiles Wunder:
> Erlösung dem Erlöser!

At the end, Christianity does not redeem Parsifal. In a sense, he redeems Christianity by surpassing the image of the historical Christ who willingly took on the sins of the world and died for them. Instead, Parsifal is redeemed in the very flesh, here on earth, *alive*.

The venerable Romantic problem of re-entry is also solved. The restoration of the lost spear, and its lasting reunion with the Grail, forms only the visible resolution of the tension that we have perceived beginning with *The Flying Dutchman*. But Parsifal's actual salvation takes place within. For the "pure simpleton," the one who remains entirely free of social and religious illusions, learns in the end to instruct himself. When he is thoroughly self-instructed, he is able to introduce new value into the Christian society of Monsalvat because he has discerned the meaning of its traditional guiding symbols, and has learned how they can be used. It is exactly the way Wagner uses them before the Bayreuth audience in his Festspielhaus.

Parsifal's redemption, his last stage of self-instruction, is clearly at hand when he regains control of the spear; for the spear, as Peckham points out, " is Wotan's spear, with a difference. It symbolizes power, to be sure, but not power over others; rather, power over the self, control of identity through insight, an insight, it must be remembered, made possible by means of the power of empathy." [17]

The concluding portion of Wagner's ten-act drama—a drama that begins with *The Flying Dutchman*—can scarcely claim to be Christian, even though, as in the case of *Tannhäuser* or *Lohengrin*, it was intended to function within a Christian context. The philosophical and religious background of *Parsifal* may best be seen as eclectic: pagan, Christian, Hindu, and Buddhist. Each ingredient is skillfully blended under the spell of Arthur Schopenhauer's salient tenets of human compassion and empathy, but carefully salted to Richard Wagner's own taste.

In *Parsifal*—in the final analysis—Wagner substitutes art for religion. If we recall the beginning of the essay *Art and Religion*, set down in 1880 when the musical execution of his last work was nearly completed, we see that Wagner there let us discern exactly what he was up to. "One could say that when religion becomes artificial," he wrote, "it remains for art to salvage the true essence of religion by perceiving its mythical symbols—which religion would have us believe to be the literal truth—only according to their figurative value, in order to make us see their profound, hidden truth through idealized representation." [18] Obviously, Wagner knew what he was talking about.

Was Wagner a Christian to begin with? The German philoso-

pher Friedrich Nietzsche, who supported him closely for years,
but later—after the *Ring* performances of 1876—began to turn
against him with venom, claimed that he was. Nietzsche insisted
that in his final work the erstwhile "master" had hopelessly "sunk
at the foot of the Cross." Despite his brooding enmity, however,
the philosopher of the new atheism could scarcely refrain from
extolling the Christian attributes of *Parsifal.* In 1887, after hearing
the Prelude for the first time, Nietzsche wrote to his sister Elisabeth that "when listening to this music one lays Protestantism
aside as a misunderstanding." [19] It must be admitted that Nietzsche never fathomed the truth. Much nearer to the truth is the
view of Morse Peckham, who believes that "Wagner, like Parsifal,
became a Christian only in the sense that out of pity for men he
pretended to share their illusions so that he might free them." [20]

In the end it is only Wagner's art, the music itself, which redeems, for it justifies the significance of religious illusions on
stage, just as it provides the ultimate source of any experience of
value. The Christian Monsalvat, whose leaders clearly have failed,
is saved by Parsifal, yet only in so far as he gives its floundering
society the *opportunity* for self-redemption. Surveying his work
during his very last days, Wagner himself forcefully underlined
this fact. Writing to Heinrich von Stein on January 31, 1883—a
mere two weeks before his death in Venice—Wagner tells his
friend: "If we cannot save the world from its curse, then we can
reveal at least vivid examples that lead on to the most profound
intuition of the possibility of salvation." [21]

CHAPTER 7

Wagner and Wagnerism

D ESPITE his sizeable contribution to the realm of ideas in the nineteenth century, it is solely as a musician that Richard Wagner had a strong and explicit impact on the culture of the West. His influence upon the course of music throughout the final portion of the last century and during the early decades of our own is immense.

Few critics will agree with the opinion that the development of opera, as we recognize it now, would have remained the same without Wagner. It could easily have succeeded without him, and in all likelihood it would have succeeded very well. Yet if Wagner had never lived, most operas written after 1870 would scarcely have sounded as they do sound. A host of composers, major and minor—and by no means all of them operatic—were significantly affected by Wagner's musical presence. Richard Strauss, Gustav Mahler, Anton Bruckner, and the early Arnold Schönberg in German, Debussy and Saint-Saëns in France, Puccini, Mascagni, Montemezzi, and Zandonai in Italy, and in Russia both Tschaikovsky and Rimsky-Korsakoff, stand out as cogent examples. But the list could be easily extended.

Quite specifically, most of the works of Richard Strauss, who was once referred to as "the second Richard," and important operas such as Debussy's *Pelléas et Mélisande* (1902), Camille Saint-Saëns' *Samson et Dalila* (1877), Puccini's *La Fanciulla del West* (1910), and Rimsky-Korsakoff's *The Invisible City of Kitezh* (1907), would all have been unthinkable in their present form if Richard Wagner had never existed.

But that is hardly all. For if Wagner's symphonic stance toward the lyric stage, together with his novel harmonies, can be seen to have guided the hand of numerous composers of opera and descriptive music, his influence extended a long way into wholly non-musical regions as well.

130

In regard to the generation that matured after 1875, both the style and the subject matter of drama, poetry, and prose not infrequently came under his sway. The writers of that generation, and even of later ones, were dominated primarily by the Wagnerian idea of "a total work of art," known in German as the *Gesamtkunstwerk*. This concept which, in theory at least, sought to fuse, within the theater, the arts of music, poetry, dramatic action, scenery, and the dance, in addition to elements from the plastic arts, proved to be as persuasive to the imaginations of some poets and dramatists as the theory itself was quite beyond realization, even by Wagner himself.[1]

Wagner's fascinating notion, nevertheless, was able to entice with its theory what it could not do in fact. The important later plays of August Strindberg (1849–1912) and those of the Belgian Maurice Maeterlinck (1862–1949), for example, together with most dramas of the French Symbolist school, reveal a good deal of what can be termed Wagnerian influence. In the words of Haskell Block, these dramatists endeavored "to approximate the grandiose conception of the Wagnerian opera," and sought "to compose a drama of operatic structure, marked by long scenes, expansive dialogue, and strained and extravagant passion, set forth in passages of luxuriant poetry or highly colored prose."[2] Plays such as Maeterlinck's *Pelléas* and Strindberg's *A Dream Play* (1902) and *Swanwhite* (1902) exemplify this trend better than any others written at the turn of the century.

Ultimately, these dramatists were attracted not only to the notion of employing literary symbols in the same manner in which Wagner used musical ones (his system of "leading motives," or *Leitmotive*); they were also strongly impressed by Wagner's creative reinterpretation of ancient myth, by which he seemed to lay bare the intrinsic nature of human existence in history and to reveal the truth of our mortal condition through the penetrating eye of musical and literary symbols.

The most original exponent of Wagnerism, however, and the most fruitful continuation of Wagner's symbol system, is not to be found in the drama at all, but rather in the prose of Thomas Mann (1875–1955). For him, Wagner remained a lifelong intellectual romance, and he happily conceded the fact. Wagner's influence on both the style and the content of much of Mann's best work is almost legendary.

If the probing analysis of Wagnerian character and the lucid perceptions about Wagner's art in Mann's essay of 1933, "The Sufferings and Greatness of Richard Wagner," have scarcely been surpassed, Wagner's imprint on Mann's fiction is as solid as it is renowned. This is apparent, above all, in the characterization and the themes of his outstanding novels *Buddenbrooks* (1901) and *The Magic Mountain* (1924), not to mention the subject matter of such stories as *Tristan* (1903), *Blood of the Volsungs* (1905), and *Death in Venice* (1911). In addition, Wagner's music itself, particularly that of *Tristan und Isolde*, points up the truth of what might be termed "Mann's Law," his metaphor of art-disease-death, a metaphor signifying the inevitable alienation of the artist and his work.[3]

Yet the first prominent intellectual to become thoroughly sensitive to Wagner's esthetic pulse was, ironically perhaps, not a German. Born more than half a century before Thomas Mann, Charles Baudelaire (1821–1867) may be considered the initial literary figure of importance to give full recognition to Wagner as an original renovator in art. Baudelaire's attitude gradually began to be shared by great numbers of people inside European cultural circles during the generation after his death. The French journal *Revue wagnérienne*, for instance, first saw the light in 1885.

But in 1861, having been exposed to representative selections from Wagner's works in concerts, and finally to the new "Paris Version" of *Tannhäuser* (in March of that year), Baudelaire maintained that Wagner's music induced him as an artist to behold novel visions and colors lying quite beyond the poet's expressive power. These visions could be revealed at most, he claimed, by way of an analogous literary symbolism. The Symbolist dramatists and the poet Stéphane Mallarmé were later to accept Baudelaire's proposal at face value. What Baudelaire saw, and what the Symbolists did, more men of letters were soon to do—from G. B. Shaw to T. S. Eliot and from Swinburne to James Joyce—in their individual way, when they beheld for themselves how Wagner invested the ancient heart of legend with a fresh, magic vision, and how he regarded the archetypes of the human condition through a modern creative eye.

The English, no less ardently than the French, espoused Wagnerism with a profusion of literary reflections and allusions, beginning with Charles Swinburne's "Wagner Poems" of 1883 and continuing with Aubrey Beardsley's Wagnerian illustrations of the mid-1890's, with specific, if sportive, references in a play or two by Oscar Wilde from the same period, and, in 1898, with G. B. Shaw's fascinating critical study entitled *The Perfect Wagnerite*. If such signs of Wagnerian influence seemed impressive in the last century, the examples of T. S. Eliot and James Joyce in our own are equally so. Wagnerism in Eliot's *The Wasteland* (1922) certainly appears significant, if hardly pervasive; however, in the major novels of the Irishman James Joyce, whose love of Wagner's music dramas increased as he grew older, variegated Wagnerian strands are interwoven.

Yet Wagnerism, unhappily, also found less than gratifying expressions in the course of the twentieth century. The whole Wagnerian exterior, its ostensible Germanness, the heroic dimensions of its stage and its music, in addition to Wagnerian thoughts about the basic soundness of the German race and the less than meritorious qualities of Jews and Latins, all became amplified and distorted by the grim pilots of National Socialism, encouraged by their leader Adolf Hitler, whose adoration of Wagner's music dated from his twelfth year. Hitler's admiration for *Die Meistersinger* especially knew no limits; it is said that he saw it performed at least two hundred times.

The Nazification of Richard Wagner, particularly of *Die Meistersinger*, which was officially looked upon as "the most German of all German masterworks," during the years between 1933 and 1945 reached characteristically excessive proportions soon before the end of the Nazi period. In the summer of 1943, and within the space of scarcely more than three weeks, Wagner's music drama about Nuremberg and its Hans Sachs was presented sixteen times at Bayreuth for the edification of Nazi potentates, including Hitler himself, as well as for that of nearly thirty thousand officers, convalescing troops, and munitions workers. The entire Nazi rationale behind this special "War Festival" was thoroughly elucidated in a popular book issued precisely for the occasion and called *Richard Wagner und seine Meistersinger.*[4]

Nowhere are the perverse sentiments toward Wagner harbored by the men who ruptured the world better exposed than in statements like the following: "If Adolf Hitler has recognized the necessity of guiding the German people back to the self-awareness of their unique essence and their destined mission, which is the struggle against baseness and against all evil in the world, he has similarly uncovered in Richard Wagner's brilliant life-creations the large artistic medium by which the German, and the task assigned to him by providence, becomes symbolized. Through Richard Wagner's creations, in the loftiest form and language to be sure, the German continually reveals himself, his nature and aspirations, his capabilities and his consciousness of duty." [5] For several decades in the mid-twentieth century, such attitudes had a pernicious effect on Wagner's reputation among large groups of people throughout the non-German world.

Not only the genocidal psychotics of Nazidom, however, mis-employed the idea of "Wagner" or some of the notions it seemed to represent. Writers in various media, guilelessly enough, have often looked upon the terms "Wagnerian" or "Götterdämmerung" as epithets or figures of speech in order to use them, far beyond their literal sense, as metaphors that suggest the violent grandeur of nature, or else to convey a mood of final catastrophe. They have appeared so profusely and indiscriminately in this fashion that these words have become proverbial.

Examples range all the way from *Time*'s gratuitous reference to "the lowering summer skies of Moscow burst with a Wagnerian thunderclap, lightning bolts crackled among the onion domes of the Kremlin," to herald Charles de Gaulle's arrival in Russia in June, 1966,[6] to Evert Sprinchorn's remark in the Introduction to his edition of Strindberg's Chamber Plays. Describing the closing episode of *The Pelican*, Sprinchorn imaginatively writes that after the alcoholic son sets ablaze his childhood home, there ensues, "a domestic Götterdämmerung that announces the bankruptcy of the family as an institution and the end of bourgeois drama." [7]

These examples reveal that Wagnerism—whether in journalism, politics, literature, or music—has come to thrive permanently in the Western world, quite independently of the original context of Wagner's personality and his work. Thus, even though Wagnerism has long been a minor vogue and has grown into a classic reference, especially for musicologists,[8] we can legitimately look for the essential Wagner once again. We might then hope to discover who the original Wagner actually was.

The poet-musician himself, however, may be held in some part responsible for the cloud of conflicting emotions and comments that has so often obscured the true image of his personality and art. When his days were waning, when *Parsifal* was gradually taking shape, and his health—frequently questionable—began to disclose gloomy signs, a veritable mystique started to sprout about Wagner and Bayreuth.[9] Rather than deploring this cult of his personality and his art, as Nietzsche and the anti-Wagnerians were soon to do, Wagner did nothing to stop it. He even assisted, perhaps innocently, in its cultivation. This cult has, in any case, survived him; and its signs have not yet disappeared. But today, the Wagnerians as well as the anti-Wagnerians are beginning to seem old-fashioned. Needless to say, they have hardly succeeded in clarifying the real Wagner.

A truly significant part of the real man and artist is illuminated in one of Wagner's own statements, which specifies what he felt to be the meaning of his individuality and his creations. The year he was in Venice at work on the second act of *Tristan*, becoming all the while ever more engrossed by notions that were to provide the whole gist of his final drama, Wagner wrote to Mathilde Wesendonk about his freshest intuitions regarding compassion and empathy, feelings which are expressed by the word *Mitleid*.

"This compassion," Wagner informs Mathilde in 1858, "I recognize within me as the strongest fiber of my moral being, and it is undoubtedly this which is also the fountainhead of my art. . . . I am not speaking here of what another suffers, but rather of what *I* suffer when I know him to be suffering. . . . In this manner, my own empathy transforms the torment of another into a reality, and the less significant the creature with whom I am able to empathize the broader and more embracing becomes the circle wherein my sensitivity is engaged. In this fact, however, lies that characteristic of my personality that appears to other people as a weakness." [10]

It is precisely this "harmony in compassion" (*Übereinstimmung im Mitleiden*) that Wagner looked upon as the only source of genuine happiness. His view reveals a dominant trait of a personality which, we recall, was already explicitly shown at a rather early stage of his artistic evolution—long before he became familiar with Arthur Schopenhauer's opinions on the subject of *caritas*, and before his own dramatic crystallizations of the notion of *Mitleid* in the *Ring* and in *Parsifal*. As early as *The Flying Dutchman*, when Senta encounters the alienated mariner for the first time, we remember her pondering whether "the voice of *Mitleid* could deceive" her. In *Parsifal*, written nearly forty years later, compassion and empathy are revealed as practically the only kind of human behavior which proves capable of ultimately surmounting the world's most beguiling illusions, as well as its real torments. As Wagner demonstrates vividly time after time, it is through the insight provided by empathy and compassion alone that one is able, in the end, to perceive eroticism as a snare, and all of social power as a horror.

It is this instinct, this compassionate understanding for "the error of existence," as Wagner once called it, that guides his artistic personality, just as it glows in the bright center of each one of its offspring, pervading the bone and marrow of them all beneath the sonorous majesty of their tonal cosmos.

Yet Wagner's permanence—that part of him which will be known and loved in the future—does not lie here. His most abiding virtue will always be his music; for it is the most accessible of the arts, in the same way that it is also the least accessible to mundane or casual criticism. As to the past, Wagner's appeal to the future will derive from the sensuous cloak of sound that engulfs and conceals his astonishing labyrinth of thoughts. This is so because, in the final analysis, Wagner is successful at nothing so much as being able, in the words of Thomas Mann, "to breathe into life and make popular the highly intellectual in the guise of an orgy of the senses." [11]

Wagner's non-musical preeminence, on the other hand, and his transcendent cultural importance rest on rather different ground. With singular perceptiveness, Mann was able to circumscribe that cultural fundament upon which Wagner's permanence stands firmest, where his major work appears, indeed, to be "the German contribution to the nineteenth-century tradition of monumental art, which in other nations assumes, from first to last, the form of the great social novel. Dickens, Thackeray, Tolstoi, Dostoevski, Balzac, Zola—their works, all of them crowned by the same urge for moralizing grandeur, are the very essence of the *European* nineteenth century with its literary social conscience and its spirit of social criticism." [12]

Richard Wagner's total significance, therefore, is twofold. It seems fated to remain a striking but disparate combination, a perplexing yet enduring union of two vast spheres.

Notes and References

Chapter One

1. In the lengthy autobiography *My Life*, which he dictated to Cosima in the years 1865–66, Wagner describes this youthful experience as follows: "There soon arose within me an image of the most sublime, supernatural originality (Beethoven) with which nothing could be compared. This vision merged with that of Shakespeare: in ecstatic dreams I encountered them both, beheld them and spoke to them; on awakening, the tears streamed from my eyes." *Mein Leben* (Munich, 1911), I, 41.

2. Wagner finished the scoring on March 1, 1833. It is published in Volume XII of the Collected Edition of his works.

3. E. T. A. Hoffmann, in his story "The Poet and the Composer," suggests the blending as well as the interaction of the world of fantasy with that of reality for the purposes of opera. This notion influenced the composer's own concept. Features of Wagner's version were also derived from the eighteenth-century fable *La Donna Serpente* by the Italian playwright Gozzi.

4. It was first produced in Munich in 1888, and has since been revived on occasion.

5. Until Wagner's being rescued financially, in 1864, by Bavaria's King Ludwig II, ending his financial worries for the remainder of his life, the composer's nearly constant indebtedness proved a hazard both to himself and, for other reasons, to his more generous friends.

6. For an exhaustive discussion of this entire episode see Chapter thirteen in Volume I of Ernest Newman's *The Life of Richard Wagner* (New York, 1933).

7. Professor Earl Wasserman of Johns Hopkins implies—and this author agrees—that the seminal cultural problem of the Romantics was "that they all face the central need to find a significant relationship between the subjective and objective worlds." See "The English Romantics; The Grounds of Knowledge," *Studies in Romanticism*, IV (1964), 33. Before Heine and Wagner conceived their versions of an alienated, subjective hero who sought to make some sense out of the

objective world through the figure of the Dutchman, other important Romantics, such as Byron in *Manfred* and Coleridge in *The Ancient Mariner,* had confronted a similar problem in the same way.

Chapter Two

1. According to the report of Mrs. Schmole who, as an adolescent, was in the audience at the première, it was only the choruses for the sailors and the spinning-maidens that generated enthusiasm, in addition to certain lyric moments in Act Two. "Compared to the heaven-storming *Rienzi,*" Mrs. Schmole wrote in her Reminiscences of 1895, "the success of the *Dutchman* showed a certain contrast. . . ." *Letters of Richard Wagner: The Burrell Collection* (New York, 1950), pp. 123–124.

2. Boito with his *Mefistofele* and *Nerone,* in addition to Leoncavallo with such operas as *I Pagliacci* and *Zaza* are rare exceptions.

3. Thomas Mann, *Wagner und unsere Zeit* (Hamburg, 1963), p. 79.

4. *Ibid.,* p. 71.

5. Morse Peckham, *Romanticism* (New York, 1965), pp. 18–19.

6. For a thorough examination of Wagner's sources, see Ernest Newman's *The Wagner Operas* (New York, 1949), pp. 3–23.

7. Arthur Schopenhauer, *Die Welt als Wille und Vorstellung* (Leipzig, 1908), I, 444. My translation.

8. Wagner changed the title after learning, as Newman points out, "that certain ribald wits were giving too Rabelaisian a sense to the earlier title." Newman, *Life,* I, 332.

9. It is certain that in the years 1848–1851 Wagner was an avid reader of the German philosopher Ludwig Feuerbach, as well as an enthusiastic exponent of key points of that philosopher's thought. The tacit atheism found in a work like *The Essence of Christianity* must not have been lost on Wagner. In addition, the style of Wagner's *The Art-Work of the Future* has been seen to bear strong likenesses to Feuerbach's own style. See Newman, *Life,* II, 431 (Note).

10. "Das mittelalterliche Gedicht brachte mir den Lohengrin in einer zwielichtig mystischen Gestalt zu, die mich mit Misstrauen und dem gewissen Widerwillen erfüllte, den wir beim Anblicke der geschnitzten und bemalten Heiligen an den Heerstrassen und in den Kirchen katholischer Länder empfinden." *Gesammelte Schriften und Dichtungen,* ed. Wolfgang Golther (Berlin, 1913), IV, 288.

11. *Schriften,* IV, 302.

12. In contrast to "diatonic," which signifies the predominant use of whole tones of the musical scale, "chromatic" refers more often than not, to the use of the half tones, or accidentals, in this scale. Wagner used it to characterize the sensuous, the erotic, and the

human. It occurs first in the *Tannhäuser* Overture and the Venusberg scene.

13. Morse Peckham, *Beyond the Tragic Vision* (New York, 1962), p. 248.

Chapter Three

1. The first sketch concludes with the notion that the gods, in the words of Ernest Newman, "are free henceforth to rule the world and lead it upward in growth of moral consciousness—which had been their desire and purpose from the beginning." Newman, *The Wagner Operas*, p. 398.

2. "Mit meinen dichterischen Conzeptionen war ich stets meinen Erfahrungen so weit voraus, dass ich meine moralische Ausbildung fast nur als von diesen Conzeptionen bestimmt und herbeigeführt betrachten kann. Der fliegende Holländer, Tannhäuser, Lohengrin, Nibelungen, Wodan,—waren alle eher in meinem Kopf als in meiner Erfahrung." *Richard Wagner an Mathilde Wesendonk*, ed. Wolfgang Golther (Berlin, 1904), p. 97.

3. "Wodan und die Wala— Schuld der Götter, und ihr nothwendiger untergang: Siegfrieds bestimmung— Selbstvernichtung der götter." *Skizzen und Entwürfe zur Ring-Dichtung*, ed. Otto Strobel (Munich, 1930), p. 67.

4. *Richard Wagner an Frau Julie Ritter* (Munich, 1920), p. 90.

5. Wolfgang Golther states that the myth of the World Ash in this form is completely Wagner's own, and considers this whole mythological picture to be "anschaulich und bedeutungsvoll." See "Anmerkungen zu Band 6," X, 86 and 91, *Schriften*, ed. Golther.

6. Peckham, *Vision*, p. 251.

7. Edward Downes in his introduction to *The Ring of the Nibelung*, (New York, 1960), p. xi.

8. "Schlimm steht's um euch Götter, wenn ihr verträgen lügt; schlimmer um dich wahrst du den reif; langsam nahet euch ein ende, doch in jähem sturz ist es da, lässt du den ring nicht los!," *Skizzen*, p. 227.

9. "Fricka's Verachtung vor den helden, die für sich ja garnichts seien, sondern alles nur durch Wodan." *Skizzen*, p. 239.

10. "Doch sie alle, die menschen, hängen im götternetz: was wir ihnen bestimmt (sic!), thun sie einzig: ihre thaten wirken sie auf unser geheiss. . . . O könnte ich alles götterthum in einen samentropfen drängen, aus dem ein freier mensch entsprosse! so möchte ich das götterthum vernichten." *Skizzen*, p. 241.

Chapter Four

1. "Der Tristan ist und bleibt mir ein Wunder! Wie ich so etwas habe machen können, wird mir immer unbegreiflicher: wie ich ihn wieder durchlas, musste ich Auge und Ohr weit aufreissen," *Richard Wagner an Mathilde Wesendonk* (Berlin, 1904), pp. 242–43.

2. Ernest Newman, *The Life of Richard Wagner,* II, 590.

3. Newman, *Life,* II, 522–23.

4. The complete passage runs in the original: "Doch entsinne ich mich, schliesslich meine Absicht gewaltsam einmal zur Geltung gebracht zu haben, und zwar . . . in der tendenziösen Schlussphrase, welche Brünnhilde an die Umstehenden richtet, und von der Verwerflichkeit des Besitzes ab, auf die einzig beseligende Liebe verweist, ohne (leider!) eigentlich mit dieser 'Liebe' selbst recht ins Reine zu kommen, die wir, im Laufe des Mythos, eigentlich doch als recht gründlich verheerend auftreten sahen." *Briefe an August Röckel von Richard Wagner* (Leipzig, 1894), pp. 67–68.

5. "Ausser den Nibelungenstücken habe ich noch einen *Tristan und Isolde* (die Liebe als furchtbare Qual) . . . im Kopfe." *Briefe an Röckel,* p. 72.

6. Morse Peckham, *Beyond the Tragic Vision* (New York, 1962), pp. 256–57.

7. *Ibid.*

8. In *Madame Bovary* (1856), the French novelist Gustave Flaubert effectively demonstrated, in his own way, what Wagner was revealing in *Tristan* and *The Ring.* Flaubert shows how Emma Bovary gradually learns to perceive both sentimental religion and transcendental romance as destructive illusions.

9. *Das Rheingold* and *Die Walküre* had already been performed in Munich, in 1869 and 1870 respectively.

Chapter Five

1. *The Concise Oxford Dictionary of Opera,* ed. Harold Rosenthal and John Warrack (London, 1964), p. 430.

2. Wagner's use of the technical and artistic terms of the Mastersingers' Guild, together with the versification forms and popular expressions of sixteenth-century Nuremberg, are wholly authentic. The dramatist's major sources were Jacob Grimm's "Über den altdeutschen Meistergesang" (1811) and Wagenseil's *Von der Meistersinger holdseliger Kunst* of 1697, from which Wagner took elaborate notes in the Vienna Royal Library.

3. "Mann könnte sagen, dass da, wo die Religion künstlich wird, der Kunst es vorbehalten sei, den Kern der Religion zu retten, indem sie die mythischen Symbole, welche die erstere im eigentlichen Sinne

als wahr geglaubt wissen will, ihrem sinnbildlichen Werte nach erfasst, um durch Ideale Darstellung derselben die in ihnen verborgene tiefe Wahrheit erkennen zu lassen." X, 211.

4. "Diese edle Täuschung, dieser Wahn muss . . . aber vollkommen aufrichtig sein; er muss sich von vornherein als Täuschung bekennen." VIII, 28.

5. "Die Nichtigkeit der Welt, hier ist sie offen, harmlos, wie unter Lächeln zugestanden: denn, dass wir uns willig täuschen wollten, führte uns dahin, ohne alle Täuschung die Wirklichkeit der Welt zu erkennen." VIII, 29.

6. *The Tragic Vision*, pp. 259–60.

7. "Wahnfried" is the name Wagner himself bestowed on his home in Bayreuth (see Chronology). Its approximate meaning is "freedom and repose from both deception and illusion."

Chapter Six

1. *König Ludwig II und Richard Wagner: Briefwechsel* (Karlsruhe, 1936), III, 182.

2. Even though Wagner in his own version broke decisively with the medieval traditions of the Parsifal legend—represented by Chrestien de Troyes and Wolfram von Eschenbach—when he equated the bleeding lance with the spear of Longinus, thus connecting the wound of Amfortas with that of Jesus on the Cross, it is patent that from his voluminous readings on the subject he was well acquainted with the medieval tradition of the maiming of Amfortas in the groin. From Wolfram von Eschenbach's long epic, which had been gestating in his mind ever since 1845, Wagner was certainly familiar with the fact that Amfortas had turned mortally sick from the wound in his groin caused by a heathen's poisoned spear. That this tradition obviously played a role in Wagner's ultimate conception of the drama is explicitly shown by the way in which he associates the spear with eroticism, and in the way he juxtaposes Kundry with Parsifal through that spear, as well as in the manner in which he connects the wounded Amfortas with the self-emasculated Klingsor. The reason why Wagner chose not to make the wound's location explicit on stage requires no comment. That in Wagner's imagination this "wound" was clearly erotic in its origin is apparent from the note following.

3. The original passage reads: "Genau botrachtet ist Anfortas der Mittelpunkt und Hauptgegenstand. Das ist denn nun aber keine üble Geschichte. Denken Sie um des Himmels willen, was da los ist! Mir wurde das plötzlich schrecklich klar: es ist mein Tristan des dritten Aktes mit einer undenklichen Steigerung." *Richard Wagner an Mathilde Wesendonk* (Berlin, 1904), p. 144.

4. *Die Briefe Richard Wagners an Judith Gautier* (Zurich, 1936), p. 164.

5. During his mature years Wagner became an ardent student of the occult and religious philosophies of the East; particularly after his growing enthusiasm for the writings of Schopenhauer, who was himself an admitted Buddhist. Wagner's strong interest in, and sound knowledge of, Oriental thought is revealed in his sketch for a Buddhist drama called *Die Sieger* written in May, 1856. Some of its ideas were later to be embedded in his rich conception of Kundry. Wagner's own Buddhist orientation is further attested to by his leadership in the German Humane Society, as well as by his embracing vegetarianism late in life.

6. The German text reads: "Kundry hat von ihrem Verhältnis zu Amfortas kein Bewusstsein. Dieses kommt ihr nur im 2. Aufzug bei den Worten: 'Zeigest du zu Amfortas mir den Weg'; deshalb soll Kundry hier nicht aufmerksam zuhören." *Parsifal,* Edition Peters, p. 51. In the Peters edition of the vocal score appears the statement that these extra notations, added above the vocal line, "correspond to directions given by Wagner personally." Ostensibly, these notations represent Wagner's final thoughts about his material. Future references to comments in the vocal score refer to this Peters edition.

7. Quoted from Ernest Newman, *The Wagner Operas* (New York, 1949), p. 662.

8. *Ibid.,* pp. 662–663.

9. "Parsifal ist ganz in dem Zustand, in dem er Amfortas gesehen hat." Peters Edition, p. 378.

10. Curt von Westernhagen, *Richard Wagner* (Zurich, 1956), p. 365.

11. See note 6.

12. "Was zwischen allen vorgeht, ist ein ungeheures Geheimnis; man weiss nicht, ob Parsifal Kundry erkennt oder nicht." Peters Edition, p. 504.

13. Peckham, *The Tragic Vision,* p. 262.

14. "Im dritten Aufzug bei der Taufe wird Parsifal wirklich zum Stellvertreter des Heilands." *Gesammelte Schriften und Dichtungen,* ed. W. Golther, X, 172.

15. Paul Henry Lang, "Parsifal Hush: Pious Delusion," *New York Herald Tribune,* April 2, 1961.

16. *Ibid.*

17. *The Tragic Vision,* p. 261.

18. See Chapter 5, note 3.

19. Quoted from Newman, *Wagner,* IV, 545.

20. *The Tragic Vision,* p. 263.

21. "Können wir die Welt nicht aus ihrem Fluch erlösen, so können

doch tätige Beispiele der ernsthaftesten Erkenntnis der Möglichkeit der Rettung gegeben werden." *Gesammelte Schriften und Dichtungen,* X, 321.

Chapter Seven

1. Wagner laid down the foundations of his theory in his two long essays *The Art-Work of the Future* (orig. German ed. 1849) and *Opera and Drama* (orig. German ed. 1851). The relation of the arts is thoroughly explored by Jack Stein in his *Richard Wagner and the Synthesis of the Arts* (Detroit: Wayne State University Press, 1960).

2. Haskell M. Block, "Strindberg and the Symbolist Drama," *Modern Drama,* V (1962), 317. See also Elliott Zuckerman, *The First Hundred Years of Wagner's Tristan* (New York, 1964), pp. 83–122, for a complete discussion of this matter.

3. All of Thomas Mann's specific pronouncements on Wagner are to be found in *Wagner und unsere Zeit,* ed. Erika Mann (Frankfurt, 1963).

4. *Richard Wagner und seine Meistersinger* (Nuremberg, 1943).

5. "Hatte Adolf Hitler die Notwendigkeit erkannt, das deutsche Volk zur Selbstbesinnung auf sein ureigenstes Wesen und seine schicksalhafte Bestimmung, den Kampf gegen alle Niedrigkeit und gegen alles Schlechte in der Welt, zurückzuführen, so hatte er auch in dem genialen Lebenswerk Richard Wagners das grosse künstlerische Mittel gefunden, in dem der deutsche Mensch und die ihm von der Vorsehung gestellte Aufgabe versinnbildlicht wird. Aus den Schöpfungen Richard Wagners spricht immer, allerdings in der höchsten künstlerischen Form und Sprache, der deutsche Mensch über sich, sein Wesen, Wollen, Können und Müssen." *Ibid.,* p. 159.

6. *Time,* July 1, 1966, p. 20.

7. August Strindberg, *The Chamber Plays* (New York, 1962), p. xxiv.

8. References to Wagner's contributions to musical culture in the Western world may be found in nearly every major and minor book or article written about music or musicians during the last sixty years.

9. This cult was perceptively, if rather venomously, examined and described by Friedrich Nietzsche in his *Der Fall Wagner,* written in 1888.

10. "Dieses Mitleiden erkenne ich in mir als stärksten Zug meines moralischen Wesens, und vermutlich ist dieser auch der Quell meiner Kunst. . . . Es handelt sich hier nicht darum, was der Andere leidet, sondern was *ich* leide, wenn ich ihn leidend weiss. . . . Somit macht mein Mitleiden das Leiden des andern zu einer Wahrheit, und je geringer das Wesen ist, mit dem ich leiden kann, desto ausgedehnter und umfassender ist der Kreis, der überhaupt meiner Empfindung

nahe liegt. Hierin liegt aber auch der Zug meines Wesens, der andern als Schwäche erscheinen kann." *Wagner an Mathilde Wesendonk,* pp. 50–52.

11. Mann's phrase ("das Höchstgeistige als Orgie des Sinnenrausches zu verwirklichen und 'popular' zu machen") is found in the essay "Leiden und Grösse Richard Wagners" in *Wagner und unsere Zeit* (p. 101).

12. "Sein Werk ist der deutsche Beitrag zur Monumental-Kunst des neunzehnten Jahrhunderts, die bei anderen Nationen vorzüglich in der Gestalt der grossen sozialen Romandichtung erscheint. Dickens, Thackeray, Tolstoi, Dostoiewski, Balzac, Zola,—ihre mit demselben Hang zur moralistischen Grösse getürmte Werke sind *europäisches* neunzehntes Jahrhundert, literarisch-gesellschaftskritische, soziale Welt." *Ibid.*, p. 148.

Selected Bibliography

The literature about Richard Wagner and his art, both from a musical and non-musical point of view, is so vast that only a judicious selectivity could hope to suit the exigencies of this limited study. The present choice of secondary works is, therefore, guided by the principle of what in the opinion of the author is meritoriously comprehensive, significant, and original. Some of the material excluded from the bibliography is found in the notes; much of the rest may be run down in the bibliographies of the standard editions and the major secondary works referred to below. Editions of Wagner's scores as well as books, studies, and articles concerning the strictly musical aspects of Wagner's art are not specifically taken into account, and the student is referred to the numerous comprehensive reference works on this subject.

PRIMARY SOURCES

Bibliographies

SILÈGE, HENRI. *Bibliographie Wagnérienne française* (Paris, 1902).

BARTH, HERBERT. *Internationale Wagner-Bibliographie 1945–1955* (Bayreuth, 1956).

STROBEL, OTTO. *Richard Wagner, a Chronology* (Bayreuth, 1952).

Editions of Wagner's Literary Works

Richard Wagner's Prose Works (New York, 1966), 8 vols. Reprint of the 1896 translation by Ashton Ellis.

Gesammelte Schriften und Dichtungen, ed. Wolfgang Golther (Berlin, 1913), 10 vols.

Sämtliche Schriften und Dichtungen (Leipzig, 1919), 12 vols.

Richard Wagner. Skizzen und Entwürfe zur Ring-Dichtung, ed. Otto Strobel (Munich, 1930).

My Life (New York, 1936). Translation of the critical German edition: *Mein Leben,* ed. Wilhelm Altmann (Leipzig, 1933), 2 vols.

Letters

Letters of Richard Wagner. The Burrell Collection, edited with notes by John N. Burk (New York, 1950). Heretofore entirely unknown or suppressed letters and documents.

Altmann, Wilhelm. *Richard Wagners Briefe nach Zeitfolge und Inhalt* (Leipzig, 1905).

Briefe in Originalausgaben (Leipzig, 1912–1919), 9 vols.

Briefwechsel mit Franz Liszt (Leipzig, 1919), 2 vols.

Briefe an Theodor Uhlig, Wilhelm Fischer, Ferdinand Heine (Leipzig, 1912).

Briefe an August Röckel von Richard Wagner (Leipzig, 1894 and 1903).

The Letters of Richard Wagner to Anton Pusinelli (New York, 1932).

Richard Wagner an Minna Wagner (Berlin, 1908), 2 vols.

Richard Wagner an Mathilde Wesendonk, ed. Wolfgang Golther (Berlin, 1904).

König Ludwig II und Richard Wagner: Briefwechsel (Karlsruhe, 1936), 3 vols.

Briefe Richard Wagners an Judith Gautier (Erlenbach, 1936).

Wagners Briefe an Frau Julie Ritter (Munich, 1920).

Richard Wagner an Theodor Apel (Leipzig, 1910).

Les Lettres françaises, special ed. (Paris, 1935).

Briefe an Hans Bülow (Jena, 1917).

Richard Wagner an Mathilde Maier (1862–1878), ed. Hans Scholz (Leipzig, 1930).

Bayreuther Briefe 1871–1883 (Berlin, 1907), 2 vols.

Briefwechsel mit seinen Verlegern, ed. Wilhelm Altmann (Leipzig, 1911), 2 vols.

Wagners Briefe an Freunde und Zeitgenossen, ed. Erich Kloss (Leipzig, 1912).

SECONDARY SOURCES

ADORNO, THEODOR W. *Versuch über Wagner* (Frankfurt a. M., 1952). One of the better critical approaches to Wagner's cultural position.

BARTH, HERBERT and WILLY HAAS. *Bayreuth in der Karikatur* (Hamburg, 1957). A history of Wagner's theater in caricature from the 1870's until the mid-twentieth century.

BARZUN, JACQUES. *Darwin, Marx, Wagner* (New York, 1958). A major study dealing with the three trailblazers of the nineteenth century and their cultural significance for our own. Not without prejudices where Wagner is concerned.

BEAUFILS, MARCEL. *Wagner et le wagnérisme* (Paris, 1947). A history of Wagnerian influences upon the arts in France.

BENTLEY, ERIC. *The Playwright as Thinker* (New York [Meridian

Books], 1957), pp. 87 ff. Bentley demonstrates that *Tristan* is *not* a tragedy.

BERTRAM, JOHANNES. *Mythos, Symbol, Idee in Richard Wagners Musikdramen* (Hamburg, 1956). A modern approach to Wagner's use of "myth" and "symbol."

BOUCHER, MAURICE. *The Political Concepts of Richard Wagner* (New York, 1950). A detailed analysis of Wagner's thoughts about politics and their influence on Nazi Germany.

CHAMBERLAIN, HOUSTON STEWART. *Richard Wagner* (Munich, 1896), tenth edition 1940. The comprehensive treatment of Wagner's thought in connection with his art is harmed by the writer's bias.

DONINGTON, ROBERT. *Wagner's "Ring" and its Symbols* (New York, 1963). The most recent and thorough approach to the meaning of symbols in the tetralogy.

FEHR, MAX. *Wagners Schweizer Zeit* (Aarau, 1934–1954), 2 vols. Wagner's lengthy residence in Switzerland 1849–1872 is examined from various angles.

FERGUSSON, FRANCIS. *The Idea of a Theater* (New York, Doubleday [Anchor], 1953), pp. 80–109. *Tristan* is discussed from the point of view of modern myth and dramaturgy.

FÖRSTER-NIETZSCHE, ELISABETH. *The Nietzsche-Wagner Correspondence*, trans. by Caroline V. Kerr (New York, 1921).

FRIES, OTHMAR. *Richard Wagner und die deutsche Romantik* (Zurich, 1952). A discussion of the "Romantic" sources and connections of Wagner's work.

GOLTHER, WOLFGANG. *Richard Wagner als Dichter* (Berlin, 1904). One of the best early studies of Wagner as a poet and dramatist by a foremost Wagner specialist.

GUTMAN, ROBERT W. *Richard Wagner. The Man, His Mind, and His Music.* (New York, 1968). Wagner's work as seen in relation to his private life and to the cultural and political climate of late nineteenth-century Germany.

HERZFELD, FRIEDRICH. *Minna Planer und ihre Ehe mit Richard Wagner* (Leipzig, 1938). A documentation of Wagner's first marriage (1836–1857) from Minna's point of view.

D'INDY, VINCENT. *Richard Wagner et son influence sur l'art musical français* (Paris, 1930). An examination of Wagner's influence on French music by one of France's most prominent composers.

ISPER, KARL. *Richard Wagner in Italien* (Salzburg, 1951). Wagner's attitude towards, and creativity in, Italy.

JÄCKEL, KURT. *Richard Wagner in der französischen Literatur* (Breslau, 1931), 2 vols. Review of the chief propagandists for Wagner in France.

KREOWSKI, ERNST and EDUARD FUCHS. *Richard Wagner in der Karikatur* (Leipzig, 1907). Lengthy textual clarifications accompany the depiction of Wagner and his works in caricatures, as these appeared in the European press from 1856 to 1907.

LORENZ, ALFRED. *Das Geheimnis der Form bei Richard Wagner* (Berlin, 1924–33), 4 vols. A significant contribution to the study of dramatic and musical structure in Wagner's works.

LOOS, PAUL ARTHUR. *Richard Wagner. Vollendung und Tragik der deutschen Romantik* (Munich, 1952). Wagner is presented as the guiding spirit and culmination of German Romanticism.

MANN, THOMAS. *Wagner und unsere Zeit,* ed. Erika Mann (Frankfurt a. M., 1963). Contains all of Mann's utterances about Wagner in letters, essays, and pamphlets.

MAYER, HANS. *Richard Wagner* (Hamburg, Rowohlt, 1959). Mayer's presentation may stand as one of the most critical and up-to-date evaluations.

MOOS, PAUL. *Wagner als Ästhetiker* (Berlin, 1906). Wagner is seen as an esthetician.

MOSER, MAX. *Richard Wagner in der englischen Literatur des 19. Jahrhunderts* (Berne, 1938). Wagner's art and his esthetic theories as reflected in English literature.

NEUMANN, ANGELO. *Erinnerungen an Richard Wagner* (Leipzig, 1907). The man who first produced the *Ring* outside of Bayreuth reviews his association with Wagner and his work.

NEWMAN, ERNEST. *The Life of Richard Wagner* (New York, 1933–1946), 4 vols. Newman's is recognized as the definitive biography. In their enormous comprehensiveness and detail, the four volumes can be said to surpass most other biographies preceding them, just as they supersede the writer's own earlier studies: *Wagner as Man and Artist* (New York, 1925) and *Fact and Fiction about Wagner* (London, 1931).

———. *The Wagner Operas* (New York, 1949). The best study to date on the sources for Wagnerian drama.

NIETZSCHE, FRIEDRICH. *Schriften für und gegen Wagner* (Leipzig, 1924). Nietzsche's attitudes in essays for and against Wagner are here presented and reviewed by the philosopher's sister Elisabeth.

PECKHAM, MORSE. *Beyond the Tragic Vision* (New York, 1962). Peckham presents a fresh and pertinent view of the meaning of Wagner's works within the general context of the nineteenth century.

RAYNER, ROBERT. *Wagner and "Die Meistersinger"* (London, 1940). A lengthy scholarly treatment of the background, inception, and development of Wagner's opera.

RÖCKL, SEBASTIAN. *Ludwig II und Richard Wagner* (Munich, 1920), 2 vols. A first-hand documentation of Wagner's Munich years.

SHAW, GEORGE BERNARD. *Major Critical Essays* (London, 1948). Contains the classic Shavian pronouncement on Wagner in the essay "The Perfect Wagnerite."

SHAW, LEROY R. "The Noble Deception: 'Wahn', Wagner, and *Die Meistersinger*" *Monatshefte*, LII (March, 1960), 97–111. A critical examination of Wagner's text and his dramatic idea from the standpoint of cultural symbols.

SKELTON, GEOFFREY. *Wagner at Bayreuth* (New York, 1965). A complete chronicle of Bayreuth, its productions, problems, and personalities, from 1872 until the present. In general, this supersedes most of the earlier histories.

SIEGFRIED, WALTER. *Frau Cosima Wagner* (Stuttgart, 1930). A biography of Wagner's second wife and her reign over Bayreuth from 1883 to 1906.

STEIN, JACK M. *Richard Wagner and the Synthesis of the Arts* (Detroit: Wayne State University Press, 1960). An evaluation of the legitimacy of Wagner's "total artwork."

STEIN, LEON. *The Racial Thinking of Richard Wagner* (New York, 1950). An interesting, but rather irrelevant, study of Wagner's views on Germans, Latins, and Jews.

TAPPERT, WILHELM. *Richard Wagner im Spiegel der Kritik* (Leipzig, 1903). Wagner's image and works as reflected by nineteenth-century critics.

VIERECK, PETER. *Metapolitics. From the Romantics to Wagner* (New York, 1941). A classic of anti-Wagnerism in the 1930's.

WAGNER, SIEGFRIED. *Erinnerungen* (Stuttgart, 1923). Memoirs of Wagner's son.

WAGNER, WIELAND (Editor). *Richard Wagner und das neue Bayreuth* (Munich, 1962). Essays by various writers on postwar Bayreuth.

WESTERNHAGEN, CURT VON. *Richard Wagner: Sein Werk, sein Wesen, seine Welt.* (Zurich, 1956). A comprehensive biography of Wagner's creations and their milieu.

——. *Vom "Holländer" zum "Parsifal"* (Freiburg, 1962). Wagner's major works are surveyed as a unit.

WOOLLEY, GEORGE. *Richard Wagner et le Symbolisme Français* (Paris, 1931). A meritorious study of the Wagnerism of the French Symbolist school.

ZUCKERMAN, ELLIOTT. *The First Hundred Years of Wagner's "Tristan"* (New York and London, 1964). The most laudable and exhaustive study of Wagnerism and Tristanism up to this time.

Index

151